why i hate
green beans

why i hate green beans

and other **confessions**
about relationships, reality tv,
and how we see ourselves

Lincee Ray

Revell

a division of Baker Publishing Group
Grand Rapids, Michigan

Published by Revell
a division of Baker Publishing Group
PO Box 6287, Grand Rapids, MI 49516-6287
www.revellbooks.com

Printed in the United States of America

Library of Congress Cataloging in Publication Control Number: 2017039109

18   19   20   21   22   23   24   7   6   5   4   3   2   1

For Mama—a lover of green beans

Simple Disclaimer

Even though my mama suggested I "call them out," I'd like to formally announce that some of the names of people in this book have been changed to protect the ones who can't help but act like jack wagons. I also collected consent forms from friends I mentioned, in exchange for withholding embarrassing stories from the manuscript. Let the record show that money was never exchanged, just favors.

However, if you or someone you Snapchat happens to personally know, sort of know, or is friends with the CrossFit trainer who was slightly disappointed but mostly pleased with the *Gilmore Girls* revival and sounds exactly like one of the people described in my book, none of this is personal and I'm sure they are all lovely people.

Contents

Contents

Introduction

I May Hate Green Beans, but I Love Oreos

can't recall the first time I tried green beans, but I do know I have decided to hate them forever. Sure, they smell like feet, but the unappealing aroma has little to do with my aversion. I hate green beans because my mom made me eat them to lose weight.

Once I hit puberty I pretty much lived in the curvy category of life. I was the epitome of a boisterous lyric by Sir Mix-a-Lot and oddly unfazed by this fact. This puzzled my tall, thin mother. Why would anyone embrace a figure that wasn't exactly like Twiggy's from the sixties?

If I've learned anything over the years, it's this: the majority of women on the planet struggle with a variety of insecurities.

Our skinny jeans deceive us.
Our grandmothers' cold cream regimens torment us.
Our Facebook feeds taunt us with images of everyone else's picture-perfect lives.

I wrote this book to encourage women everywhere to embrace the days when we aren't feeling like our best selves. It's for everyone who's tried the latest fad diet or online dating app and failed—again. It's for those of us who scour the internet looking for ways to reduce stress, only to roll our eyes when we discover step one is always the same: cut out the caffeine.

As if that's going to happen.

We long for someone who's been there to walk close to us through life's difficulties. I know what it's like to laugh uncontrollably about insecurities. I also know what it's like to hurt deeply because of those same inhibitions. Much like our favorite bras, we women must lift up each other in a spirit of camaraderie. Whether about maneuvering the muffin top, navigating the sketchy waters of singleness, or walking the judgmental halls of the workplace, these stories are my way of sharing certain truths I've learned along the way and found incredibly helpful.

Yoga pants are your friend, Jesus sees you, and green-bean diets are never the answer.

mirror, mirror on the wall

Seasonal-themed Oreos are one
of God's greatest gifts.

1

Why Is Charlie Brown's Teacher Talking to Me?

I had the coolest language arts teacher in the eighth grade. Not only did Mrs. Smith make studying grammar, composition, and public speaking a fun activity, but she also took the time to invest in our lives. Her assignments were creative and entertaining, and they often involved her students really digging into their tender junior high brains, forcing us to take a good strong look at who we currently were as well as who we wanted to be.

One homework assignment involved designing a coat of arms to represent different phases of our lives. Mrs. Smith presented us with six prompts, and each answer had to be expressed through a drawing. I recently found the folder with my coat of arms proudly displayed on the front. With great humiliation I share my results of that assignment with you now.

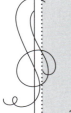

1. What was the most significant event in your life?

I drew Mickey Mouse ears. The most significant event in my fourteen years of life was that one time I went to Disney World when I was eleven years old. The seed was planted early, friends. I love Disney.

2. Draw your happiest moment in the past year.

I drew a piece of paper with the words *math test* on it and a 100 written in red at the top. The happiest moment of eighth grade was making a perfect score on a pre-algebra test. Math was difficult for me in general, and it became a sensitive topic in my world. I strongly believe the hours I spent trying to learn the area of a triangular prism contributed to the love and dedication I have for the characters on *The Big Bang Theory*.

3. Indicate something at which you are good.

I was good at holding purple pom-poms. I absolutely loved being on the cheerleading squad, but I'd like to point out that a flawless math test trumped making cheerleader as my happiest moment that year.

4. What is something you are striving to become or be?

Without a doubt, Young Lincee was striving to one day make the Hallsville Bobcat Belle drill team. No contest.

5. If you had one year to live and were guaranteed success in whatever you attempted, what would you attempt?

First, that's a little morbid, don't you agree, Mrs. Smith? Second (I am not making this up), I drew a scale with the arrow pointing to ninety pounds. I surrounded the scale with Dr Pepper bottles and Hershey chocolate bars and wrote, "I would eat fatty foods and not gain weight."

6. If you died today, what three words would you most like to be said about you?

"I liked her."

In summary, my coat of arms epitomized a girl who loved Disney, experienced major anxiety about perfection, longed for a stage, was fiercely self-conscious about her weight, had a minor Dr Pepper addiction, and desired for people to like her above all else.

At times today, that coat of arms is a clone of what it was decades ago. I find myself battling the same insecurities I did in Mrs. Smith's class. Fortunately, I have a healthier perspective on life—and work that affords me the opportunity to go to Disney World.

I didn't always drag around these insecurities. When I was young, self-doubt never occurred to me. I was rarely unsure. I performed for my family, my friends, my dolls, the dog, the horses, whoever was driving the car, patrons in the grocery store, a brick wall, and the imaginary audience in my huge backyard. I spent days making up routines in the swimming pool, on the trampoline, in roller skates, or on the picnic table. It's what I did. It's who I was.

Someone should have intervened the summer of 1980 when I constantly sang the entire soundtracks from *Annie*, *Grease*, and *The Sound of Music* against the balcony in the living room as though I were a miniature Evita. I was obsessed with a little redheaded orphan, an Australian Goody Two-Shoes hopelessly devoted to a T-Bird, and solving a problem like Maria. My outbursts of song and dance didn't seem to bother my parents or my sister. Mama and Jamie had even been known to join in a time or two. Daddy would emphatically roll his eyes and turn up the volume on the TV.

Performing is in my DNA. My extended family embraces the stage because life doesn't make sense without one. My grandmother designs dance costumes for a living. Most of my aunts and cousins have old megaphones in their closets that are frequently utilized. That's why they are in the closet and not the attic—easy access. Give any one of the Ray women a baton and she'll immediately launch into a routine from days of yore. Give that same baton to me and I will use it to knock some object off a high shelf.

It wasn't until puberty kicked in that I experienced my first bouts of insecurity. I became conscious of my peers watching me and deduced they probably had opinions about what they were seeing.

Do they like my dance moves?

Do they appreciate my ability to rock a mic like a vandal?

Do they think I'm stupid?

Are they laughing because of how my cheerleader uniform fits?

When did we inaugurate a popular crowd, and what does "two-faced" mean?

Weren't we all friends last week?

Overnight, I morphed into an introvert who was often mistaken for an extrovert. If you put me on a track that encircled a football field, I could easily bust out a crowd-pleasing cheer and have a blast doing it. But you wouldn't expect me to make eye contact with you in the hallway, because I would hate to disrupt your between-the-bells rhythm and accidentally make you late for class.

The same is true today. If I walk into a party crowd, I find a nice spot near a vertical surface and remain stationary for the duration of the merriment, which, fingers crossed, is hopefully a come-and-go affair. I try to provide amusement to anyone who dares approach the weirdo wallflower. Never presume I freely mingle with other guests like a civilized human being. I must be physically pulled by the arm toward the person you want me to meet—that is, if I haven't already snuck out the back door.

Season two of *New Girl* introduced me to the life-altering genius that is the Irish good-bye. Thanks to Nick Miller's reclusive ways, I have since mastered the art of removing myself from a social situation with little to no farewell. Please understand that I will stealthily seek out the host of the gathering and genuinely thank him or her for including me on the invite list. My mother and Emily Post didn't raise a monster. But the rest of you jokers will probably receive a nice text explaining my whereabouts or never hear from me at all. This mysterious character trait is part of my charm.

If, however, I have a designated role in entertaining or educating that same crowd, I do the exact opposite. Put a microphone in my hand and I'm unstoppable. Offer me a headset like the one Britney Spears wears and I will regale you with tales and include wild hand gestures and comedic facial expressions. Give me a podium and I'll abandon my notes midspeech. I thrive on improvisation and have often been known to go rogue.

What's that you say? Your emcee bailed and you need someone to run the show on a moment's notice? Take me to your event and allow me to save the day.

This gregarious character trait is part of my charm too.

I desperately want to be seen. And at certain times I am equally terrified that will happen. I live with the constant nag of my introvert side begging me to blend in while my extrovert side craves to tag a conversation with the perfect sarcastic comment. It's a peculiar juxtaposition.

The need to perform often wins out. It's in my blood and can't be stopped. I guarantee if you look through a microscope at the chromosomes that make up my genes, they will be positioned in a perfect pyramid, wearing rhinestone headbands.

My people are dancers, twirlers, gymnasts, and cheerleaders. That eighth-grade coat of arms correctly foreshadowed my trying out and later securing a spot on the Hallsville Bobcat Belle drill team my sophomore year of high school. I couldn't wait to put on my uniform with the sparkling overlay full of purple and gold sequins, as well as my brand-new white boots. I practiced kicking my leg high enough to touch the brim of my hat. I soaked up every eight-count, every practice, every routine, and every second on the football field. This was where I was meant to be.

What I didn't love was being measured and weighed on Mondays. Did I ever consider this tradition an incredibly antiquated practice? Nope. I accepted Weigh Day as the bane of my existence. That horrific chart in our director's office mocked me every single week. It said I was five feet two with small bones, therefore I should weigh 108 pounds.

Interesting. I was a fifteen-year-old girl with muscular legs and a "healthy" derrière, and some doctor in a book published in 1974 thought I should weigh what I had back in fifth grade. Why, this made perfect sense!

The green beans first appeared when it was reported that the extra four pounds of insulation I was carrying around declined to budge. Mama believed with all her heart that green beans contained supernatural enzymes that promoted weight loss. She still does. She has personally experienced the phenomenon on more than one occasion, and she was perfectly willing to buy as many cans of this vegetable as needed to melt away the unwanted excess around my haunches.

Mama loves a green bean. Ordinary people eat them sautéed, caramelized, bacon-wrapped, roasted, casseroled, or barbecued. Unfortunately, these recipes are chock-full of extra ingredients that counteract the weight-reducing molecular structure found in the bean itself. Mama prefers to eat them straight out of the can; therefore her daughters would eat them straight out of the can. I always complained that they smelled like a boy's locker room and tasted like sweaty socks.

She popped them like Tic Tacs.

I had to put my foot down the day beets established a regular rotation in my diet. I believe any food that stains a paper plate shouldn't be introduced into my digestive system. Mama obliged and simply doubled up on my green bean helping. She also suggested I pack some green beans and maybe a chicken breast or two for my lunch the next day. I started crying.

Trying to be incognito about an air-based diet in the high school cafeteria is no easy task. While other girls ate their Wonder Bread sandwiches, nacho cheese Doritos, and cinnamon-flavored Teddy Grahams, I attempted to look cool choking down my rice cake with a SlimFast chaser. There's nothing like the chalky aftertaste of a French vanilla bean shake to get you through an afternoon slump.

After a year dancing on the drill team line, my dream was to prove myself worthy of becoming a lieutenant. Officer tryouts were looming, and I began to get nervous. You see, for every pound over your ideal weight, you received a demerit. For every demerit you incurred, points would be taken off your final score at tryouts. I hovered around 112 and cursed those extra four pounds every time I stepped onto the scale. I needed a new strategy. Something different.

Enter the cabbage soup diet.

Lord, help me. If green beans are the smelly feet of all garden crops, then cabbage is the stinky armpit of the edible plant world. This diet was sweeping the nation and promised a ten-pound weight loss in only one week. As I lifted the lid to peek at the limp cabbage, tasteless celery, and pathetic tomatoes bubbling away in a huge pot, I immediately deduced this particular food blend had to be a distant relative of the hot mush Miss Hannigan served the orphans.

Annie was right. It is a hard-knock life.

My sister and I hated this soup so much we poured the concoction into a blender so we could trick our brains into adopting the myth that it was a smoothie. A brown, gritty, disgusting smoothie. Mama drank it as though it were going out of style. Of course she did.

When the week of tryouts arrived, I was still a great big chunk (eye roll) at 111 pounds. Nothing was helping me lose the weight. No amount of Jane Fonda workouts could suppress my fear that I would be docked three points on my final tryout score. My dream of trading in my purple uniform for a white officer uniform was coming to a close.

The night before the big day, Mama came to me holding a tiny pill in the palm of her hand. "Swallow it," she said. "This will help you." I didn't hesitate. I examined the object, chucked it into my mouth, and waited for her to explain the anticipated effects of the magic capsule I had ingested.

I feel as though I need a disclaimer here. I am a child of the eighties, and I want to formally announce that the DARE program worked on me. I said nope to dope. I preferred hugs over drugs. I wasn't one to hoover pills for the fun of it. It's different, however, when your prescription medication provider is your own mother. She had to take matters into her own hands.

Mama called for reinforcements, and that came in the form of a spare water pill from the secret stash of a good friend. Mama explained that all the excess water I may be retaining would be evacuated over the next several hours. Who needs sleep when drill team tryouts are in the morning? Desperate times call for desperate measures.

I went to the bathroom seven times in twelve hours that night. I woke up feeling refreshed, energized, relatively lighter, and ready to conquer the scale as well as my solo. *Let's do this.*

I skipped breakfast, because any rational person would know eating a healthy meal before a long day of tryouts would utterly counteract the desired effects of all that excess water being eliminated from my system. Mama dropped me off at the school, and I immediately hightailed it to the scale and begged my director to weigh me. I was down to 107 pounds. *Oh happy day!* Had cell phones existed back then, I would have taken a selfie and posted it on all social media platforms. #blessed

I ran off to find my best friend, Julie, in the hallway. She was super excited to hear I had miraculously lost the weight. We started warming up, and minutes later we were escorted into the gym to perform the standardized team routine in front of the judges. The next round was the high kick line. Then we waited for callbacks. All that took about four hours.

Around lunchtime, I specifically recall Julie offering me some Cheese Nips from a plastic baggie. I resisted the temptation. One Nip would make me bloated. I refused to chance it. Instead I adjusted my glorious red, white, and blue stars-and-stripes overlay that perfectly symbolized my patriotic-themed solo, set to the classic tune of "Yankee Doodle Dandy." My prop was one of those white wooden guns the girls in the flag corps spun.

Can you tell a bunch of family twirlers helped me choreograph this routine? *Here's hoping I nail my toss turnaround, and God bless America.*

I performed my solo and squealed with Julie as she finished hers. Then we marched in one by one for our interviews. One judge suggested, "Using the letters of your name, describe yourself with adjectives." My knee-jerk reaction was irritation. I have not one, but two *e*'s in my name. That's a hard letter, and this entire exercise suddenly seemed unfair. I took a beat—smiling, of course—to collect my thoughts and answered Lovely, Intelligent, Normal, Creative, Elegant, and Effervescent. I thought I did a pretty good job. Poor Alexis is probably still sitting in that gym trying to come up with an *x* word.

We quickly changed back into our basic leotards for another few rounds of dance and high kicks. We waited for our turn in the hot hallway and then burst through the doors into the cold gymnasium. Back and forth. Round and round. The judges kept mixing us up in groups of five, trying to determine who would prevail at the end of the day as Bobcat Belle officers.

We had just performed the routine known as "the strut" and were poised at attention as the judges wrote down their comments, when my exciting day started to go south.

I was standing still in drill team position. My head was high, my smile was big, and my vision was uncharacteristically blurry. I squinted my eyes and glanced at Julie. *Why on earth would the judges need to see us in dim lighting? And what's that drumbeat? Did the band come to prove we can dance to their music? Oh wait. That's my heartbeat thumping in my ears.*

Suddenly I realized the judges were talking, but I couldn't understand. Trust me when I say Charlie Brown's teacher is real and she lives in the form of a woman from Jacksonville, Texas, who judges drill team competitions. I turned my ear to try to decipher the "wah, wah, wah, wah" language, but I came up short.

Let me be clear. Not once did I ever deliberate, "What's going on with me?" I took the darkness, the phantom Bobcat band, and Charlie Brown's teacher as standard operating procedure. Much like the N in my name, they were completely normal at the time.

Julie was directly to my right. I got the sense she was worried about me, but I didn't know why. As I looked at her, she was telling me with her eyes that I should be moving. I looked to my left, and the girl who had previously been right there seconds ago was halfway to the door. I started to follow, feeling sluggish. I kept telling myself to smile. That's the last thing I remember before slamming into a wall and falling onto the gymnasium floor.

Perhaps I should amend that "intelligent" adjective from my name?

I woke up to Charlie Brown's teacher, another judge, and my director clapping their hands and slapping me on the face. Someone kept shouting, "Honey? Are you okay?" I looked up, confused, and immediately blurted, "Please don't make me do a callback! I can't do it!" and mumbled something about Cheese Nips and how I love being from the land of the free and the home of the brave. I'm quite sure Charlie Brown's teacher shares my story at conventions and parties.

I'm proud to inform you I did make officer that eventful day. So did Julie.

I should also share that those pesky five pounds came back almost immediately. My grandmother had to make me a new white uniform because the school didn't own any that fit my body. Much like Shakira's hips, my hourglass figure did not lie.

Sometimes I want to take that lovely, normal girl and hold her in my arms and tell her she is so much more than a number on a scale. I want her to embrace the curves and the muscles. I want her to freely eat those Halloween Oreos.

I want her to know I see her struggle, and I want to tell her it's going to be okay.

2

36 x 24 x 36 (Only If She's 5'3")

A collective group of you are currently thinking, *What kind of Polly Pocket drill team line didn't have an officer uniform big enough to fit an average-sized high school girl?*

I understand your confusion. But it wasn't my weight that hindered me from shimmying into that idolized snowy white leotard. It was my ample bosom. My boobs were too big to zip up the darn thing. No amount of stuffing, adjusting, or basting would do the trick. Once again I was the laughingstock of my peers.

The first time my boobs were a problem was during my aforementioned days as a junior high cheerleader. I was the tallest girl on the squad. I was the base of every pyramid. I was the reason we couldn't wear our purple crisscross squad uniforms for away games. My solid C-cup interfered with the middle two buttons. While other mothers were taking in the waists of their daughters' skirts, mine was buying a minimizer bra.

I see some of you rolling your eyes. I get it. The grass is always greener, am I right? Allow me to paint a picture of what it was like for me to be a busty gal.

If I bought a dress that fit my top half, the bottom half was way too big. My entire wardrobe had to be different-sized pieces that could be purchased separately. One time I went shopping for a formal dress for the eighth-grade dance. Department stores didn't sell any two-piece options. I considered not attending the function because my dress was so plain. One-piece bathing suits were a nightmare. Had "saddest memory" been an option on Mrs. Smith's coat of arms exercise, this would have been a close second to what came next.

I was notified that the guys in my grade had unanimously voted me the "biggest boobs" recipient during athletics that day. My male informant didn't quite compute why this news cut me to the core. We were in the throes of adolescent discovery! A few of our friends had already paired up and had been "going" together for weeks. This placed me squarely on the cusp of the popular group bubble, and if I played my cards right, he guaranteed I could have a boyfriend by the end of seventh period.

He was disappointed when I didn't celebrate with a victory bounce. Pun intended.

The idea of boys noticing me and my body that way was unsettling. Not only did I have to worry about the other cheerleaders whispering behind my back, but now I had the entire baseball team talking about my boobs. As a sweet, naive kid, I didn't know how to properly handle this sticky situation. I immediately adopted a concave posture. I rolled my back and pushed my shoulders forward, forcing the illusion that my figure was more of a blob than like Marilyn Monroe's. It's hard not to be noticed when you have the body of a full-grown woman with the innocent face of a young girl who simply wants to listen to her New Kids on the Block cassette tape on her Walkman in peace.

Take that humiliation and multiply it by one thousand. That's the uneasiness I felt when I had to wear an extra-large leotard a few years later at drill team practice. I remember the facial expressions, giggling, and intimidating eye contact of the three girls who welcomed any chance to verbally make fun of my massive chest. They openly laughed and pointed at me. One noted that my execution of the routine was good, but it was too bad my huge boobs pulled focus.

The mean girl giveth and the mean girl taketh away.

The day my white officer uniform didn't zip was painful. It was hard to be comforted by Julie when all I saw huddled in the dressing room were fellow officers who were easily ten pounds lighter than me with normal-sized boobs. At sixteen, I filled an H-cup bra. I was heading into my junior year, as well as the general direction of Dolly Parton's signature trademark. I could not let that happen.

Luckily, I had a plan.

That night, I talked to my mom about getting a breast reduction. I don't remember how I even knew the term *breast reduction* or when I came up with a list of sensible facts that supported my case. I do remember the foreboding "go talk to your daddy" command that ended our conversation. If Daddy agreed, Mama would make it happen.

Johnny Ray is not a man of many words. This worked in my favor that day. It was also fortuitous timing that he was in his happy place, burning a pile of brush. The problem that faced me was my intro. How in the world are you supposed to ask your dad if you can have permission to chop off some of your boobs? Countless hours of reading Sweet Valley High books did not prepare me for this dialogue. What would Elizabeth Wakefield do?

Daddy was adamant at first. He believed God made me with big boobs and that's how it should be. It wasn't until I started tearing up that he put the lighter fluid down beside the Mason jar of loose matches and truly started listening. I told him my back ached all the time. My shoulders had dents in them. I didn't like the way boys stared at me, and I was constantly bullied by girls on the drill team. More than anything, I wanted to perform and I couldn't do that to the best of my ability with this gigantic barrier in my way. I physically hurt. I was emotionally spent. My boobs were upstaging me in life. I had a solution, and I wanted to take the next steps to get that ball rolling.

My sweet father hugged me and gave me permission to have the surgery. Then he got into his Jeep with the dog and asked that we never speak of this again.

We haven't.

That summer I had the breast reduction. I walked into high school that fall semester, my back straight as an arrow. Classmates admired me for "slimming down" over the break. I was even showered with compliments on my supercute bra in the drill team dressing room. For the first time in years, I wasn't wearing a plain cotton lunch-lady brassiere with five hooks clutching together for dear life.

This was also about the time I was openly obsessed with Disney's *Beauty and the Beast* animated feature. Is it any wonder that I identified with this story about the difference between what we put out there for others to see and who we truly are on the inside? Being seen for who I was? That's all I ever wanted.

Yes, in this scenario, I am the beast. I'm totally cool with that.

I count having a breast reduction one of the best decisions I've ever made. And even though I still struggle with other insecurities, the experience taught me not to be deceived by appearances, for beauty is found within.

3

Time Marches On
All Over Your Face

'm thankful for a few good decisions I've made along the way, because I've certainly had my share of poor ones.

I'm thinking of the summer I laid out on my friend's roof with a bottle of baby oil by my side and the musical stylings of NSYNC in my ears. I have the sunspots to prove it. Mama calls them liver spots, which annoys me to no end. It makes me sound like an old lady. I'm suddenly my great-grandmother writing a snail mail letter on pretty stationery, explaining there's no need for concern: *The liver spots have been removed and all is well. Y'all don't worry about me. I'll be fine.*

My sun spots are on my legs and arms and mercifully not all over my face. I have Sea Breeze to thank for that rarity. Much as she is with the green bean, Mama is convinced this astringent contains enchanted ingredients that promote healing. Remember how the patriarch in *My Big Fat Greek Wedding* thought Windex could cure anything? My mom is the same way with Sea Breeze. It alleviates the pain from burns, zaps zits upon contact, calms the itch of a mosquito bite, removes unwanted fingernail polish, strips the varnish on wooden objects, and is a decent alternative to hydrogen peroxide.

Word to the wise: do not use Sea Breeze as a substitute for eye makeup remover. Your corneas will burn for days and your mom won't know what to do because Sea Breeze in this instance is the unsuitable perpetrator, not the remedy.

You should know that up until recently, I never washed my face unless I was in the shower. I don't know why. It's not as though I didn't have Sea Breeze within arm's reach in every direction while I was growing up. I was blessed with great skin, and I assumed the hereditary tautness and lack of acne would last well into my twilight years. Unfortunately, no one told the bags under my eyes this was the plan.

A few years ago I called my mother in a panic. I was afraid I had contracted Bell's palsy overnight, because when I bent over to tie my shoe, my face felt like it was falling off my skull. Mama said, "That's not Bell's palsy, Lincee. That's called getting old. I told you to start using Merle Norman antiaging cold cream years ago, and you didn't listen. Welcome to your late thirties."

The bags showed up after that conversation and, to my dismay, they have been hanging around ever since. I'm extremely sensitive about them, and I can tell when they really come out to play because people ask me if I'm tired. Eighty percent of the time, the answer is yes, I am tired, because not only does your face fall off when you hit forty, but insomnia becomes the one thing you can count on. Regrettably, I feel fresh as a daisy about 20 percent of the time but folks still ask if I'm getting enough rest.

One way I attempted to combat the bags was wearing false eyelashes. Mama wore them up until a few years ago. They were a part of her beauty routine. Everyone knew this, including my aunt Shelia who once tried to kill a pair of falsies with a flyswatter because she thought they were a spider crawling on the end table.

I can still hear Mama screaming, "My eyelashes! My eyelashes are falling off!" when we were riding the Big Thunder Mountain Railroad roller coaster at Disney World. I never understood the passion behind this interjection until I had some false eyelashes of my own.

I went to a fancy place that put them on for me one lash at a time. No drugstore-box falsies for this girl. I was enamored by them. I didn't have to wear mascara. Everyone told me my eyes popped. And best of all, they totally camouflaged my bags. I even experienced my own "My eyelashes!" hysteria when I was riding in a boat around a lake with my friend Stephanie. That was the instant I officially became my mother's daughter.

After a solid summer of false-eyelash bliss, I decided the cosmetic tweak was too expensive to maintain on a regular basis. If you ran into me on the street today, you'd see my boring short lashes that in no way mask the dents under my eyes. And that's okay. I was getting a little crazy experimenting with lash length there at the end. I'd like to officially thank my friend Amy for gently letting me know I was beginning to look like a Disney princess. And not in the little-birdies-helping-me-get-dressed kind of way. My eyes were full-on theatrical and ready for their close-up.

I'm glad Amy steered me away from looking like tarantula legs were dangling from my eyelids. We need friends like this to give it to us straight. Julie once suggested I take off the gray sweater I was wearing because it made me look "a little jaundiced." I never wore that sweater again. My friend Jill used her pointer finger and thumb to pull a hair from my chin. While I was driving. How the hair was long enough to waft in the wind without me knowing it was there is not the point. Jill saw a need and she stepped in. She guffawed at the mightiness of the lone hair, placed it beside a mechanical pencil she found in the cup holder of my car to show

34

its relative size, took a picture with her phone, and then brushed it away.

We seldom speak of this incident, because Jill knows one day I'll be the one plucking a hair from her chin while she's driving.

Here's your takeaway: tweezers are your friend. I'm sure most of you have an unspoken agreement with someone you trust that she will bring tweezers to your funeral and pluck anything and everything unruly on exposed body parts, should the service be open casket. It's okay to admit you have that friend on standby. I do. Plus three backups.

I'm not exaggerating. The idea of people spotting a rogue facial hair or seeing me with unruly skin abnormalities makes my throat thick. These significant concerns stem from the events surrounding one grim afternoon. Because we are friends, I'll share the ghastly details of that infamous day.

Buckle up. I'm about to get vulnerable.

It all started with an annoying iOS update notification. These aggressive little reminders beckon us to both fear and eagerly anticipate the latest, greatest version of what new and exciting wingdings our smartphones offer. I downloaded the iOS update one quiet afternoon and spent way too many hours discovering new emojis and sending fried eggs in a skillet or a dancing lady in a red dress to various people.

I was sitting at my kitchen table, typing my text messages with my two pointy fingers. You see, I have a condition the medical community calls "toe thumbs." And by medical community, I mean the old nurse with a terrible bedside manner at my childhood pediatrician's office. Toe thumb texting is often spectacularly unsuccessful for me. There's so much meat there I tend to hit several letters instead of only one. Luckily, my friends have adapted.

There I was, punching out emojis of a lollipop and the Nicaraguan flag because it's a pretty turquoise, when a text popped up from a cute guy I knew who asked me if I wanted to buy some concert tickets from him. As I was weighing my options, my left index finger rested on a little camera icon right above the keyboard.

Suddenly, a bizarre box popped up. I saw my face—a face mere inches from my screen. Then, because the Lord knew I would one day be writing a book about insecurities, my phone took a picture all by itself.

Oh, I'm not done. Dear reader, it sent the picture by itself too.

With gut-wrenching physicality, I screamed, "NOOOOOOOOO" in my best Rachel Green voice. I sat in shock, panic, and utter despair as my face sped through the cosmos to Cute Concert Ticket Guy's phone.

I still get hives thinking about it.

For you to fully understand the gravity of this situation, it's important for me to intricately describe exactly what visual we're dealing with here. The topside of the frame caught my left eyebrow. The word *shaggy* does not even begin to describe what was going on up there. And sadly, when my eyebrows haven't been nurtured in a few weeks, the "sister scar" shows up looking worse for wear.

(Ah, yes, the sister scar. I was around three years old and was chasing my sister in the house when I turned a corner and slammed straight into a full-length mirror hanging on the back of a door. The door my sister closed so I couldn't tag her. To this day, Jamie still does not claim blame because she swears I should have seen myself coming and stopped. That cracked head is all on me.)

At this close range, Cute Concert Ticket Guy had every reason to suspect the sister scar was a result of some sort of gang initiation ceremony. He could retract his previous ticket offer for fear that hand signs might be thrown at the venue and his Live Nation account would be permanently shut down as a result.

The eccentric mole in the upper right quadrant was quite the spectacle. No one should ever look directly at it or it might steal their essence. Thankfully, the bottom of the frame ended with my chin. Or should I say chins? Did I forget to mention I was looking down at my phone? Oh yes! My phantom Bell's palsy was on full display too.

The pièce de résistance of my involuntary makeup-free selfie was definitely the "whaaaaaaat's going on?" look that accompanied the face melting extravaganza. Keep in mind that all this happened in a matter of seconds. You can imagine my butt clench when I saw the little bubbles pop up that warn your fellow texter is about to respond.

Cute Concert Ticket Guy wrote, "So, that's a no then?"

Yes, dear Cute Concert Ticket Guy, that's a no. I'm saying good-bye to future iOS updates and my dignity, as well as the fantasy of one day sharing a meal with you. I'm saying hello to my old flip phone and this coupon for Merle Norman cold cream. If you need me, I'll be over here bathing in Sea Breeze.

Baggy skin and wayward hairs can be delicate topics to some, including the person writing this book. They are the miscreants that contributed to some of the most embarrassing moments of my life. I hope my horrifying plight gives you all the confidence you need, knowing someone out there is a bigger dork than you.

4

Curl Up and Dye

*I*t's too bad Sea Breeze doesn't help your hair grow. Did I tell you about the time I was taken to the men's restroom at an El Chico Mexican restaurant because a waiter thought I was a little boy?

That was an eye-opening day.

If memory serves me correctly, I was around six years old, rocking a fresh Dorothy Hamill haircut. I'm sure my parents were trying to incite some sort of independent will in their first grader by suggesting I approach said waiter to direct me to the nearest water closet.

I knew something was up when I saw the urinals on the wall.

I used the facility, washed my hands, politely nodded to a baffled man entering upon my exit, and returned to my bean-and-cheese nachos.

I don't blame the El Chico waiter for assuming I was a boy. That I am my father's child is quite obvious. Locals and relatives used to call me Little Johnny. When my old boss first met my dad in person, he said, "It's as if someone peeled off Johnny Ray's face and put it on yours. You look exactly alike."

To which I replied, "I understand. He's one good-looking human being."

Everyone loved my Dorothy haircut. I hated it. Fortunately, Mama let me grow it out after El Chicogate, and I enjoyed the fruits of French braids and pigtails up until sixth grade.

That was the year Hot Stix entered my life.

Prepare to be shocked. My sister and I never dabbled in perms like many girls in our generation. Don't get me wrong. We may not have fiddled in front of the mirror trying to achieve five-inch bangs, but we did take the time to go big. And Hot Stix got us there.

We mercifully abandoned the dreaded sponge roller when Jamie received a set of Hot Stix for Christmas. They were long, skinny versions of hot rollers and came in two sizes, one pink and one purple. You simply twisted your hair around the rod, rolled it up to your scalp, and fastened the end of one side through a hole on the other. Once all Hot Stix were in use, Jamie resembled a stylish Medusa as she waited the designated thirty minutes for the best results.

The day I tried Hot Stix was life-changing. They were miracle workers. Like Anne Sullivan coaxing Helen Keller, these burning rods of glory somehow managed to train my hair into understanding the follicle mechanics of twisting into a coil. It took only the length of one episode of *Saved by the Bell* to produce a mass of luxurious curls. I was hooked.

Jamie used twenty Hot Stix to achieve maximum hair height and ringlet volume. I used five. Give me five stix, one pick, half a can of Rave aerosol hairspray, a hair dilly with balls on the end, and stand back as the magic unfolds.

What's that? You've never heard of a hair dilly? Allow me to expand your knowledge. Like the Hot Stix, the dilly revolutionized the curly ponytail. Everyone knows how annoying it is to pull perfect ringlets through a regular rubber band at least two times to secure a ponytail. It's a well-known fact that there's a 63 percent chance this action alone will compromise the integrity of the curlicue. Who would have the audacity to flirt with those odds? Those of you who were in dance companies or drill teams are nodding your head along with me right now.

Discovered and named by my mother, Linea Ray, the hair dilly looks like the numeral eight with plastic balls at either end. All you do is grab your ponytail, hold one ball, and wrap the other one around twice, twisting it over its mate when they meet again. There's no need to revitalize wimpy curls because they are perfectly intact. Tease away, my friend!

Like I said, sixth grade was my year. That school picture was epic. To this day I am still impressed by the circumference of the curl ball on the side of my head. My bangs had never been more symmetrical. The red hair bow complemented my red parachute pants beautifully.

That's right. I had parachute pants. In various colors. Please do not confuse these with Hammer pants, which I also owned. Parachute pants were the distant cousin of a Hefty garbage bag. They were literally made of plastic and had elastic around the waist and ankles. They looked fabulous with yellow socks and red Keds.

My earrings were pretty rad too. Middle School Lincee was a creative genius and never worried that losing one of her red heart earrings would keep her from having the perfect yearbook picture. All I needed was a paint pen, Sharpie, and a stack of index cards, and I could make my own earring. If I had been a budding entrepreneur, I would have started a custom earring business in my covered desk at the back of Mrs. Johnson's math class. Instead, I was probably asking for extra homework or anxiously waiting for a phone call from Waldenbooks, telling me the next installment of The Baby-Sitter's Club series had arrived.

I was a preferred customer.

My sixth-grade picture has forever been immortalized in the 1988 Hallsville Bobcat yearbook. It's also forever immortalized on the World Wide Web.

I never expected to receive no less than forty emails from friends, childhood classmates, and a few acquaintances who were thoroughly entertained when the aforementioned photo had been plastered all over Facebook with the teaser "27 Hilarious Kid Haircuts That Will Make You Cringe."

Excuse me?

Listen, Random Site I Never Knew Existed and I'm a Little Skeeved Out That You Have My Picture, that curly ball on the side of my head is *flawless*. Cringe worthy? Heavens no. Celebration worthy is more like it.

My appearance calmed down a bit in junior high. My curls and my wardrobe were a little more relaxed. It was loose tresses and Units for me. Units, one-size-fits-all modular pieces of clothing, were the best invention ever, and I would wear them right now if I hadn't sold them all at a garage sale three decades ago. They were the original yoga pant—*for your entire body*. A belt that can substitute for a miniskirt? I'll take one in every color.

The nineties introduced us to grunge and the magnitude of initiating flannel into our wardrobes. I fought this trend with every fiber of my being. I was comfortable in my polo shirt, braided belt, Cole Haan loafers, and denim skirt.

I remember the time I was dancing at our first senior pep rally. Directly across from me was Julie's little sister, Jennifer, and all her freshmen friends. Every single one of them had straight-as-a-board hair. Suddenly curling irons were replaced with flat irons. What was happening? Moreover, not one of the freshmen had bangs.

I experienced a hair identity crisis in college that next year. To have bangs or not to have bangs? That's the real question. I held on to them throughout college, well into my twenties. It was Julie who convinced me I needed to update my look and grow out my bangs.

To this day my forehead has been bare. I trust her completely.

I did toy with the idea of bringing them back a few years ago. I marched up to Ashlee, my current hair girl, and told her I was contemplating bangs. She sat me down and studied my head.

The relationship between a woman and her hair person is intimate. I have faith in Ashlee's judgment because she takes certain details into consideration I never do. My hair has changed over the years. It's a little bit thinner and has these infuriating wiry gray pieces that seem to be multiplying. I haven't owned a bottle of hairspray or turned on a curling iron in years. Could I pull off a straight bangs look and not appear to have a wet mop on my head?

Roughly five seconds after I sat down in her chair, Ashlee confirmed she wasn't feeling it.

So here I sit. Bangless.

I'm glad I listened to the professional, because one time Ashlee instructed me not to go dark and I made her dye my hair a chocolate brown against her will. I should have listened. I looked like an evil twin version of myself.

I find it interesting how much time I spend worrying about my body's physical flaws, when I know and believe what's inside matters most. This lesson hit home during my internship at Disney World.

Did you know an underground network spans the entirety of Magic Kingdom? It has all the amenities of a thriving theatrical community. When I was there, cast members could eat lunch in a staff cafeteria or schedule a trim at the hair salon. This was also home to the wardrobe department and the character zoo.

The dressing rooms were located somewhere below Cinderella's Castle, and my locker was near Snow White's. Her dark black wig was perfectly styled with a tiny bow. Her lips were scarlet red and her cheeks were rosy. She even had a musical voice that sounded like Snow White in the animated film. It was jarring at first to see Snow in costume from the waist up and Umbro shorts with Birkenstock sandals on her bottom half, but I got used to it.

I hate to ruin the magic for you, but there are a myriad of girls who have the face and figure to transform into each of the dozens of Disney princesses. On any given day, you could see a gaggle of Cinderellas together, walking around in house shoes. Of any three, one might be the autograph-signing Cindy, while the other two are members of the stage show or parade team.

I was told my locker-room neighbor was "A-1," meaning she was the Snow Whitiest of all the Snow Whites. If Snow White was needed for a television special or a celebrity requested a private meeting, this girl was called to fill the role.

A few weeks into my internship, Snow White and I were leaving our shifts at the exact same time. I was literally mesmerized by what I witnessed. She was wearing a purple bra with denim overalls—and no shirt. She had one yellow Converse tennis shoe and one purple. Mama always told me to match my gloves and belts to the color of my shoes. Not Snow. She matched her belt to her exposed undergarments.

She pulled off her perfectly coiffed Snow White wig, revealing massive amounts of short, dark hair with purple tips. A quick dollop of product and a few tousles later, and I'm certain Snow's spiky hair could have been used as a weapon should she encounter any evil queens on the bus ride home.

Coco Chanel said, "Once you've dressed, and before you leave the house, look in the mirror and take at least one thing off."

My Snow White would laugh, merrily of course, at this notion. Why wear one earring when you can wear seven in various styles? All you need is a teeny tiny chain that connects from one of the crosses hanging from your earlobe to the hoop in your nose. While you're at it, add two bars to your eyebrows and one in your tongue. Also, dog collars aren't just for dogs. They can look pretty cool on a princess's neck if given the appropriate scenario.

Snow picked up her backpack and offered a diminutive wave good-bye. The cartoon woodland creatures followed her out the door. I shut my gaping mouth and started getting dressed in my plain old shorts and T-shirt.

I later learned Disney talent scouts audition princesses in full costume. I was told they don't want any preconceived notions based on appearance. I have no idea if this is true today, but I approve the idea of not judging a book by its cover. Never in a million years would I have pegged the punk rocker girl as not only Snow White, but the *quintessential* Snow White. I would have seen Fido's dog collar, been concerned about her nose chain getting hung up on something, and blessed her heart for the lack of blouse.

I would have missed Snow's sweet disposition, pleasant personality, and natural ability to captivate an audience of adults as well as children.

I am my own worst critic. Most of the time when I look in a mirror, I see imperfections. I have issues with my arm flab swinging when I gesture enthusiastically. Your issue may be bird legs, or a crooked nose, or cellulite. We all have issues. But we need to remember this: "The LORD does not look at the things people look at. People look at the outward appearance, but the LORD looks at the heart" (1 Samuel 16:7).

Yes, I should start doing some sort of push-up and probably eat a vegetable more than once a week and learn to grow old gracefully. Perhaps I should reintroduce Hot Stix into my morning regime. I bet Mama still has Jamie's set and a few hair dillies in the upstairs bathroom.

I also need to recognize that my perception of my physical exterior has always been an unstable nerve Satan likes to toy with on a regular basis. He may see I am insecure about my weight, my skin, my hair, my age, and my many other flaws. But I need to remind myself who sees me as His child. I need to rest in the truth of the One who originally and so long ago instituted the idea of not judging a book by its cover.

We all do.

5

Class of 1994

Even though I still see insecurities in the mirror and time continues to march on at a rate with which I am not entirely comfortable, I've learned we must squeeze as much as we can from each day we're given.

If I could share what I know now with High School Senior Lincee, our talk would go a little something like this:

- Some of the people around you at graduation will become amazing adults. You will never see most of them again. That may make you sad now, but I've got one word for you: Facebook.
- Thank Daddy for teaching you how to fish. This pastime forges an unbreakable bond.
- Mama is right. That's the case most of the time, unless green beans are involved.
- Keep reading. It helps your writing. Maybe choose something with a little more substance than the Sweet Valley High series.

45

- Bad things happen. That's life, kid.
- You know those people who make fun of you? They're making you stronger. It's going to be okay.
- Don't be ashamed to admit your love for that guy is real.
- It's okay to be a "prude." Go ahead and own it. It doesn't change.
- Boys appreciate that you like *Star Wars*. Stop hiding your VHS copies behind *Singing in the Rain*, *Newsies*, *Princess Bride*, and *Sixteen Candles*.
- New Kids on the Block will have a reunion in twenty years and they'll be just as awesome. Your allegiance might shift a bit from Joey to Jordan, but you can claim both.
- Your DVR, iPhone, and laptop computer (yes, you own one) will be as important as air.
- Invest in those around you.
- You are beautiful. Stop worrying about your weight.
- Wear sunglasses. All the time. They help prevent excessive squinting, which gives you crow's-feet. And sunglasses make everyone look hotter.
- Apply sunscreen.
- You may think you can't handle it, but you can.
- Salsa dancing with that boy in Havana resulting in your third knee surgery will be totally worth it.
- Don't sweat the small stuff.
- Most things you sweat = small stuff.
- Don't go out of your way to avoid situations or circumstances because you're afraid of what people think.
- Travel, travel, travel, travel.
- Serve, serve, serve, serve.
- You will fall in love. With a kid in Africa.

- Making mixtapes is your spiritual gift. Start calling them playlists and you'll be cooler than your friends.
- Keep being a nerd, because nerds are awesome.
- Face it. You know what the answer is. You just don't like it. Suck it up.
- Stay frugal. You'll be debt-free because of that characteristic, and Future Lincee *thanks you*!
- Be ready to immediately respond when someone asks you to tell a joke.
- You can't erase the internet.
- Your sister is your strongest advocate and will punch anyone in the throat who hurts you. Let her.
- Your tender heart makes you compassionate and full of mercy. That's not a weakness.
- When life hands you lemons, someone will tell you to make lemonade or add vodka. That helps nothing. Amaretto sours, on the other hand, will change your life when you turn twenty-one. Trust me.
- Right now you don't understand why you interpret writing assignments differently than everyone else. That's called creativity. Don't change a thing.
- Jesus sees you.
- He can hear you too.
- Tell your story.

PART 2

she works hard for the money

I know what it means to work hard
in a man's world. I like to think I add
some sparkle to their lives.

6

There I Was, Unable to Breathe, on Peter Pan

pon receiving my bachelor of arts degree in communications from Baylor University, I drove to Florida the very next week to intern at Walt Disney World.

I was assigned to work attractions in Fantasyland and was officially bored by day three. I also developed a constant tension headache from my surroundings.

Toddlers can't help but be drawn to Fantasyland's theatrical whimsy. On a hot summer's day in August, I can guarantee no less than 150 strollers are parked outside It's A Small World, as well as 150 babies/crawlers/new walkers crying their eyes out because the family pushed them to skip their midmorning nap.

They don't show this part in the marketing videos.

Because Fantasyland is incredibly loud, a system was developed to help one cast member catch the attention of another cast member amid the joyful, laughing families documenting day one memories in the park and the miserable, wailing families trying to hold it together on day seven. Calling out someone's name or whistling morphs into a cacophony of tears and giggles. We were taught to hiss at someone if we wanted them to turn around. And I'm here to tell you this trick works. A slow and steady snake-like hiss can cut through any sound a screaming toddler or ornery kid dressed as Buzz Lightyear can summon.

To be clear, this typically doesn't work if you haven't trained yourself to listen for a hiss. Interestingly enough, it's quite easy to be trained. After two or three hisses, it becomes part of your subliminal consciousness. And it's not just a Disney World thing. I taught this trick to the girls on a mission trip, and to this day my friends Ann and Emily will whip their heads around when I hiss at them in church. They are pros.

My time in Fantasyland was short-lived. It all started the day I was on wheelchair duty at Peter Pan.

It can be argued that Peter Pan is the most popular ride in Fantasyland because it always has a long line. The ride consists of a bunch of boats that slide down a long alleyway. People jump into the boats, and then they're whisked away to Neverland. During the entire ride they look down and watch as the plot of Peter Pan unfolds.

The wheelchair entrance is on the far left—the beginning of the alleyway. This gives those who need extra help plenty of time to step onto the moving sidewalk, find their balance, and then slide into their boat. For efficient parents who have been maneuvering kids in and out of wheelchairs for years, this doesn't bother them in the slightest. And those who haven't negotiated wheelchairs still have time to figure it out before the sidewalk turns into the regular boarding. That being said, one person always freaks out.

When you work the wheelchair line, you have to walk backward on the moving sidewalk, waiting for guests to arrive. On this particular afternoon I greet a family of eight accompanying a buxom grandma in a wheelchair. I ask if they have ridden Peter Pan before. All answer in an enthusiastic chorus of "Yes!" From what I can gather, they are several generations who undoubtedly have visited the parks on multiple occasions.

At this point, it's my duty to explain exactly what will happen with the adult in the wheelchair after I confirm she can walk. They made this point clear in training, and since I'm a severe rule-follower, I take my job seriously. I follow the instructions to a *T*.

> ME: "Okay! This is going to be super simple. You're going to stand up, get your balance, and then take two steps toward me onto the moving platform. I'll hold both of your hands. You stand there and take a moment. Then I'll help you get into your boat. Easy peasy."
>
> TYPICAL RIDER: "Will the boat leave me behind on the sidewalk?"
>
> ME: "Excellent question. The answer is no. The boats move at the same speed as the sidewalk. Once you step onto the moving sidewalk, wherever you are, there's a boat right there for you. It will not leave you."

By this time the little ones are eager to get on the ride. One of the adults volunteers to go first. She shoves the kids past me and hops into a boat. A few tweens are next and I'm left with Grandma's brawny son. He helps her stand up and she grabs my hands. I can tell she's scared. I explain the instructions again, fearful that Grandma may make me look bad in front of my bosses.

> ME: "All you have to do is take two steps toward me [I say as I'm still walking backward on the

sidewalk]. One, two, and then stop. Got it? Ready?"

GRANDMA: "Yes."

The son looks unconvinced.

ME: "On three. One, two . . ."

GRANDMA: "No! I'm not ready!"

The tweens yell for Grandma to hurry up and get on the stupid ride already, because the line for Space Mountain is probably hours long by now. I try again.

ME: "On three. One, two . . ."

GRANDMA: "Don't pull me!"

I explain to Grandma that I would never pull her onto a moving sidewalk. She was going to step onto it herself. Not only is forcing Grandma to take a step a dangerous solution, but I'm pretty sure I would be fired if someone saw me. Or I'd be banished to work at the poncho stand by Splash Mountain. The horror.

The son becomes so irritated that he scoots by me and Grandma, figuring he can be more helpful if he is in a boat. Now that her son is no longer behind her, Grandma feels extra pressure to make this happen.

ME: "On three. One, two, three!"

As you may recall from my never-wavering instructions, this is the moment when Grandma is supposed to walk toward me (left foot, right foot) and then stand there. I stop walking backward because I'm supposed to let the momentum of the moving sidewalk guide her forward. We are still holding hands, yet Grandma does not take the steps. Therefore, I inadvertently pull her onto the moving platform. She lands on me. This squishy, lovely Grandma lands on me.

I am now sandwiched between Grandma and the moving sidewalk, making my way down to the general public section. I try not to waste time being frustrated at her son for chillin' in the Peter Pan boat without a care in the world. I also pray that management isn't around to see me fail miserably in this absurd moment. Trying to locate the emergency stop button clipped on my hip is a useless endeavor. It's buried, and feeling up Grandma to find it is not an option.

I decide to hiss with the hope that my general public "How many? Yellow boat. How many? Green boat" counterpart will see the error of my ways and push her own emergency stop button.

There's just one problem. When I try to hiss at the girl, Grandma's weight keeps me from properly performing my nifty trick. She's constricting my airway. All that comes out is a sputtering "sah, sah, sah, sah" sound that doesn't do anything but throw Grandma into a panic. She speculates that she's smothering me. That's when she starts apologizing profusely. Seeing that she's three inches from my face, I give her a weak smile.

After a solid thirty seconds of pseudo hissing, we finally slide up to the regular entrance. My "how many" coworker still has not noticed me. I shouldn't be mad. I would never expect her to come gliding along beside my ankles. Why should she? A man waiting in the queue says something along the lines of, "Does she need help?" before the girl punches her button. Three chivalrous Peter Pan enthusiasts lift Grandma off me. She thanks everyone involved in the rescue, squeezes my cheek, and then selects a boat from her many unmoving choices.

Those standing in line applaud me. I bow and then hide in the Pirates of the Caribbean break room.

My trip down the Peter Pan conveyer belt gave me the courage I needed to campaign for a transfer to Adventureland. There was no way things could get worse, right? My friend Jill was a world-class Jungle Cruise skipper, and we double-teamed our efforts to convince the higher ups my darling personality was currently wasted on saying to big groups of people, "How many? Yellow boat. How many? Green boat."

Jill greased the proper wheels, and after a few weeks I talked my way into Adventureland.

My monochromatic skipper costume made me look like a beige blob. I tried not to care. I was more nervous about memorizing the required long spiel. It was also rumored that Imagineers secretly rode the Jungle Cruise to make sure skippers weren't going off script. If you didn't follow the spiel exactly as it had been written, you could be fired on the spot.

I had heartburn for the first four weeks of work, but I soon settled into a comfortable rhythm once my always-follow-the-rules approach kicked into gear.

It wouldn't be the last time I leaned on my perfectionist ways to secure a dream.

7

Shunning the Dallas Cowboys Organization

After I made my mark in Orlando as a world-class Jungle Cruise skipper, I set my sights on a possibility equally as exciting: working for the Dallas Cowboys.

The Cowboys have been a constant member of my extended family for decades. My father and uncles have been known to abandon the lavishly decorated Thanksgiving table in favor of an exciting third and long touchdown pass. On more than one occasion, I flirted with the idea of trying out to be a Dallas Cowboys cheerleader. My fear of muffin top suffocated that ambition. I never embraced the team passion with jerseys, trucker hats, or foam fingers, but I did have a T-shirt claiming our boys were America's team.

My lackadaisical Cowboys fandom changed one Sunday afternoon in 1991 when a young, blond buck on the television caught my eye as he warmed up on the sidelines. His name was Troy, and I vowed to the world that I would one day be Mrs. Aikman. All

I had to do was drive my car to Cowboys Stadium, infiltrate the marketing department, and make myself available so Troy could go ahead and start falling for me. No problem.

My devotion was steadfast throughout the remainder of high school and college. When I moved to the big city to find a job in public relations, my lofty visions of Dallas Cowboys grandeur were immediately doused. It seems you can't freely waltz up to Jerry Jones and ask him for a job that places you in the general vicinity of the love of your life.

Because I needed money, I settled and took a job at an insurance company, typing in claims. A friend of a friend landed me this whimsical gig, which introduced me to the wonders of a cubicle office. Ah, the memories. I can still hear Abu trying to explain the inner workings of deductibles to a disgruntled client on the phone. If I concentrate hard enough, I can faintly smell Sandy's midafternoon squirts of her imposter designer body spray. Good times.

One day my boss plopped a fresh stack of claims on my desk. She leaned against my cubicle wall, careful not to put too much weight on the fragile structure, and praised me for the speedy rate at which I could both type and manipulate the ten-key pad. As a reward, she was giving me more work! But this project needed to be kept on the down low. I perused the stack and gasped.

I was holding insurance claims from the Dallas Cowboys organization.

No, this isn't a tell-all book where I divulge who took what pills for which ailments. My story has reached a pivotal stage. Somewhere in that building, someone had an "in" with the Dallas Cowboys, and I was going to find that someone.

It turns out it was super easy. My boss held the key to my Dallas Cowboys conundrum and arranged for me to meet with the manager of special events about a job. I chose not to dwell on the fact that she may have been trying to get rid of me and instead focused on the reality that I was about to get my foot in the stadium door. That opening might not have been Aikman's personal assistant, but it was Aikman-adjacent. I remember being the appropriate amount of nervous in the hours leading up to my interview. But I put on my navy-blue power suit and charmed my way past the first barrier. I had landed a second meeting.

The next round was a little more difficult than the friendly chat with my boss's friend. Before me perched three women with pinched-up faces, big hair, and trendy wardrobes. My exact same navy-blue suit felt a little less powerful as I sat five feet away from them, in a lone chair, under a single light, in a random room, at the stadium. Sorority bid day parties flashed before my eyes as I imagined each one of these women blackballing me for having the audacity to wear pantyhose.

Most people who interviewed me back then were enchanted by my Disney World experience. These three practically scoffed at my accomplishment. If I had to guess, I'd say they had all backpacked across Europe for a summer or maybe interned with a financial group on Wall Street. Or both. They probably ate granola and dried kale as snacks instead of Oreos.

Achieving my lofty goal of working at a theme park made famous by a mouse seemed comical to them. Even though I was highly intimidated by my potential future coworkers, I managed to convey that not only did I have the brains to do the job, but I also had a personality that embraced teamwork.

The next day I received a phone call from the triplets. The Dallas Cowboys organization officially offered me a job as an assistant sales something or other. I quit listening after the phrase "offer you a job" and started thanking them profusely. Then I began imagining my bridesmaid dresses.

Would Troy prefer silver to match that season's football helmets?

Should we blow it all out with a star theme?

Would Emmitt Smith give a toast before we danced as husband and wife to "I Swear" by John Michael Montgomery?

I suddenly realized the alpha triplet was spouting off the details about the job description. She ended her fabulous speech with the heart-stopping words, "It pays minimum wage."

She was offering me an hourly job that paid minimum wage? Clearly she did not realize I had Baylor loans that had been deferred for months.

I politely thanked the three amigos for their time and told them I would have to think about the offer, promising an answer in the morning. Then I called Daddy and straight up begged him to support me while I made a name for myself at Cowboys Stadium. He asked if we got free tickets to home games. I lied and said yes. That's when he agreed to bankroll his baby girl's delusion of being the wife of an NFL legend.

The next morning I bounded into my boss's cubicle, shared my exciting news, and officially turned in my resignation. We did a happy dance. Then I called the triplets to formally accept their offer to be an employee with "sales" in my title.

> TRIPLET: "That offer has been rescinded."
>
> ME: "I'm sorry? Don't you remember me? The girl in the navy-blue power suit?"
>
> TRIPLET: "Yes. The offer has been rescinded."
>
> ME: "May I ask why?"
>
> TRIPLET: "Because no one should have to think twice about working for the Dallas Cowboys organization."

Good-bye, Troy.

My boss was mortified. She called her friend, who was nice enough to arrange an interview with the triplets' boss the very next day so I could plead my case. This time I was escorted through the bowels of Cowboys Stadium to an ornate office well below the thirty-five-yard line. It was dark, menacing, and the triplets sat on a couch cowering before the man who came to shake my hand upon my entrance. He was holding a cigar.

And I thought the triplets were intimidating.

I tried to gather my thoughts. I could barely breathe. My dream job was on the line.

SMOKEY: "I heard we had a little mishap with your interview."

ME: "Yes, sir. I was offered a job and then the offer was rescinded."

SMOKEY: "And why do you suppose that happened?"

ME: "I was told it was because I had to think about my answer."

SMOKEY: "Exactly."

ME: "I wasn't expecting an hourly job. I called my father to see if he would help me out financially. I really want to work for this organization."

SMOKEY: "I stand by my employees. No one should have to think twice about working for us. We are the Dallas Cowboys. But this one time I'll make an exception. We'd like to offer you the job again."

I am not a confrontational person. I prefer the boat to be nice and steady. I value the difference between sarcasm and snark. However, in that split second a wave of indifference swept over my body. I looked from Smokey to his trio of uppity underlings and smiled.

Then I said, "Let me think about it."

It felt glorious. I understand now that the wave of indifference was God's protection. He provided me the courage I needed to close a door he did not want me to walk through. I hauled myself out of the gloomy office, made my way up toward the sunlight, and never looked back.

I also vowed right then and there to shun the Dallas Cowboys for thirty years. There's no reason the magic number is thirty, but my vow is unflinchingly rigid. I'm not sure what God intended me to learn, but the entire annoying experience soaked through to my bones and settled in as disgust.

Now, some of you have done the math and have keenly discovered that my Dallas Cowboys punishment is nearing its end. You're on the edge of your seats wondering if I will cease and desist from shunning should I run into Troy on the street or in an airport during my travels.

The answer is yes.

Should that happen, I will share my plight from 1999, he will laugh in all the right places, and then he'll invite me to dinner so he can hear the long version of my narrative. We will bond over our love of romantic comedies, hatred of green beans, and shared uneasiness about fourth-down conversions.

Then he'll ask me out on another date and I'll coyly respond, "Let me think about it." That answer will either charm him enough to pursue a courtship or it will be the nail in our relationship coffin. Either way, it will make for a good story. I'll let you know what happens.

8

Questionable Deli Meat

After the Dallas Cowboys undertaking, I handed my résumé to anyone with a pulse and finally landed a job at a prestigious marketing firm. Most of my accounts were in the food industry, so I spent five years shuttling people to various cooking events or prepping ingredients for live TV segments.

I worked with some high-profile chefs. Some were nice, while others took a page out of Gordon Ramsay's book. One chef asked me to get him some olive oil. Did you know Central Market has an entire aisle dedicated to just olive oil? I witnessed his fiery temper full-on when I presented him with a less-than-stellar brand.

I spent thirty minutes crying in a bathroom stall.

I also had weird anxiety about eating the foods the chefs prepared. I'm a picky eater, and no matter how pretty it looks on camera, I have no desire to eat a "refreshing fruit chutney made from watermelon and cottage cheese." However, the fear of losing my first real job because I hurt the delicate ego of a celebrity chef by not eating his masterpiece always prevailed. Bottoms up.

My time in public relations turned me into a "yes" woman. No matter what anyone requested of me, I always responded in the affirmative. I worked constantly. I was the first one to arrive and the last one to leave. Failing was not an option. I had to be the best, and I needed people to notice my hard work.

Circumstances eventually led me to move to Houston (see chapter 14), which meant looking for a new job. I quickly learned this city thrived on oil and gas. Potential employers couldn't care less that I knew chefs expect to be treated like royalty and blueberries don't look good on camera unless you grease them up with Vaseline.

I interviewed with Bill in July 2006. He flipped through my precious portfolio with the attention span of a gnat on Red Bull. He shut the book holding hundreds of my newspaper articles and slid it back in my direction with a serious question: "You don't have any oil and gas experience. Why should I hire you?"

I explained that my ability to commit to the "relations" part of public relations is the key to success. It doesn't matter if you're selling dumb iron or cast iron, blowout preventers or fried apple fritters. The foundation is the same in any scenario. Give me an audience and I will tell them what they need to know. Give me an idea and I will write a memorable piece of copy. Give me a Dr Pepper and I will have enough energy to work late hours to help contribute to the bottom line.

He hired me the next day.

I also remember the day he probably wanted to fire me. He walked into my office and said he needed me to fly to Colombia. Instead of waiting for more information, I verbally responded, "As in Ohio? I didn't know anyone was drilling in the Midwest." Bill stared at me bewildered and rebooted the conversation. He needed me to fly to Colombia, the South American country. Then he left my office, no doubt to reevaluate his decision to hire a hick from Hallsville.

At the time, it was one of my more embarrassing professional misfortunes. I texted my mother and told her Bill had asked me to go to Colombia. Before I could send the second part of my message, Mama had already texted back, "Ohio?"

The East Texas apple doesn't fall far from the tree.

For ten years I waded through the ins and outs of the industry. Having been one of only a few females in that male-dominated world, I've had my fair share of eye-rolling exploits. I've kept my face neutral as crude jokes were shared. I've tried to look feminine in flame retardant overalls, safety goggles, and steel-toe boots. I've stood before a boardroom full of men who didn't speak English, trying to convince them we didn't need to wait for my boss—*I* was the presenter.

I became proficient in all things drilling, and I quickly learned females on rig floors are about as rare as a Bigfoot sighting.

First, the whole place becomes eerily quiet. Wearing a pink hard hat only frightens them more. Once it's announced I'm there to interview the rig hands for a company newsletter, all hope is lost. Most scurry away like cockroaches while the few remaining brave ones barely make eye contact as they mumble one-word answers to my questions.

How many times have I interviewed a dude who had to stop and spit his dip midsentence? Twenty-seven. Of those times, how many swallowed that dip instead of spitting into a Styrofoam cup? Three.

The international stories are the ones I like best because they sound so exotic. I had the opportunity to travel to a handful of overseas destinations, and each time I came back with wild and crazy narratives. Then I would repurpose them when I encountered a lull in dinner conversation. One of my more notable jaunts was a facility visit in the middle of Ukraine.

Overseas traveling terrified me to no end. I never had a passport before I moved to Houston. Big outings for us growing up were a trip to Graceland and, of course, that memorable vacation to Disney World in 1986. The idea of navigating an Eastern European state all by myself resulted in some sleepless nights. I had to swallow my pride and ask a friend to walk me through everything I needed to know when landing in a foreign, non-English-speaking country.

I could not look like a fool in front of my clients.

Other than almost missing the shuttle bus to meet my colleagues at the rental car place, the trip was mostly uneventful until my last night in town. The guys from the Ukrainian company wanted to treat the Americans to a traditional dinner. Ten of us were all together at the back of a restaurant. With the Ukrainians, Russians, British dudes, Americans, and that one guy from Ghana, we were the perfect representation of a United Colors of Benetton ad. Just one girl and her entourage of rugged roughnecks. I can envision the billboard in Times Square now.

I was seated at the middle of the long table with my American colleagues on either side. The Ukrainian general manager sat across from me and motioned for the waiter to pour a round of vodka shots.

You've probably heard that Russians drink vodka like it's water. In my personal experience, I can confirm this is a true stereotype. I can also attest it's considered an insult not to drink with them. If offered vodka, you'd better partake, especially when the logistics of future million-dollar deals are circling the table.

The Ukrainian stood up and toasted everyone in the room. He spoke about the wonderful relationship between his company and the U.S. division and genuinely seemed proud to call us partners. This lasted for about five minutes. During this time, the waiter placed a plate of "something" at each end of the table. I'm no expert, but it looked like slugs.

Our host concluded his salute and pointed to the plate, explaining that this was a celebratory occasion and we would be chasing the vodka shot with herring. And onions.

I suddenly craved green beans.

The man lifted his glass and toasted the table. We all slammed our drinks back and spiked the herring with little forks. Down the hatch.

Thank goodness the vodka was like rubbing alcohol, because it burned off the aftermath of the oily, slimy, fishy taste in my mouth. It may have burned a few taste buds, too, but I was willing to receive that as a blessing in disguise.

Everyone cheered and high fived as the waiter presented a tray of cucumbers, tomatoes, and red bell peppers. I munched away. I'm a professional. I knew I could get through this, even though I can't stand tomatoes. I have the palate of a sophisticated fourth grader, but I pressed through for the good of the company.

Suddenly the waiter started making his rounds, filling the shot glasses with vodka again. Number two Ukranian guy stood up and made his own toast. It, too, lasted forever. We cheered. We clinked glasses. We took the shot. We all sucked in air afterward, like you see in the movies, before chugging yet another herring.

Soon the questionable deli meat selection arrived. Being the smart connoisseur I am, I chose the two lightest meats. I convinced myself they surely came from Oscar Mayer and mentally chanted in my head, "It's turkey and ham. It's turkey and ham. It's turkey and ham." I gobbled it up in three bites, ignoring the funny smell, only to find a plate full of rolled-up bacon thrust in my face.

You may be thinking, *Oh good! Something she recognizes. Everyone loves bacon!*

Dear friend. You are too sweet. It was bacon fat. Fat. The fat of bacon. All white, fat, bacon fat.

My Ukrainian friend called out with a huge smile, "It's good for you!" *Good to clog my arteries, but what the heck? And where's my vodka shot? Oh, here it comes!*

The waiter rushed over with a third shot. It helped to dissolve the roll of pork belly lodged in my throat.

At the beginning of the fourth course, I realized we were going to toast each dish. I tried to get the attention of the waiter, but I couldn't lift my arms. He finally realized my joints were paralyzed from the vodka and came over to see what I needed. I asked for bottled water. I kid you not, he looked me up and down as if I were from another planet. Once he understood what I needed, he brought me a bottle of plain old boring water. He knew I was a poser Russki, and I begged him with my eyes not to rat me out.

Everyone devoured the potato ravioli (not the real name, but that's what I called it) and luckily, they never noticed me pouring water into my shot glass. The next course materialized, and I enthusiastically toasted everyone. By the end of the night, the Russians were toasting the vodka, the Brits were toasting the Americans who carry guns, the Americans were toasting the Revolutionary War, and nine men were toasting the little blond girl who could hold her liquor.

All together there were seven courses. I had three vodka shots and four waters. I slept like a log that night. I also suspected my insides had been thoroughly cleansed. It's a good thing, too, because I later found out the questionable deli meat was donkey tongue.

Any time I hear a Russian accent, my arms get heavy and it's a good forty-eight hours before I can eat a turkey sandwich again.

9

Taking a Deep Breath

There I was, dreading HUET class, also known as Helicopter Underwater Evacuation Training.

Earlier that week, Bill informed me I would be going to Brazil with him to visit a few offshore rigs. He politely waited for me to finish singing a few bars of the "Welcome to Rio" song from my Disco Mickey Mouse cassette tape I wore out during the entirety of my childhood. Then he delivered some disturbing news.

> BILL: "Before we go, we have to take a HUET class. That's where they dunk you under water and you have to escape out of the helicopter simulator. You okay with that?"
>
> ME: "Sure thing."

Step one: Avoid looking like a fool in front of my boss.
Step two: Research this HUET business.

As I waited for YouTube to load my search parameters, I convinced myself it wasn't going to be that bad. I love to swim. I can hold my breath like a champ. This was going to be a piece of cake.

Then I watched the video. The guy climbed into the simulator chair. Easy enough. Then he buckled himself in. That was sort of creepy, but I got it. I watched him execute some sort of hand signal. Note to self. Then I witnessed the contraption dunk the dude *upside down*.

I did not see that coming.

I took cleansing, deep breaths to get my heart rate down. In through the nose. Out through the mouth.

Our class was in Galveston. By the time we made the hour-long trip there, I'd conjured up images of a dark simulator with five or six guys in scuba gear ready to rescue me should I start flailing about in a panic. *What if I can't hold my breath that long? What if I pass out and they have to do CPR? What if I'm the first one to ever fail HUET? What if I'm unable to go to Brazil?* The likelihood of me ever getting another chance to belt out "Welcome to Rio"—in Rio—was slim to none.

The one silver lining was my HUET wardrobe. It turns out a swimsuit falls under the forbidden clothing category. *Praise Jesus!* The only attire you need for a stranger to dunk you into a tank filled with murky water is steel-toe boots and orange-colored coveralls three sizes too big.

The class was small. I arrived with my boss and our videographer, and we were put in a room with about ten other people.

Jim, the trainer, had done this for a long time, evidenced by the way he outlined "all you need to know" about HUET safety. He demonstrated the seat belt and crossing your hands over your chest. Logistically, a helicopter has two exits—the windows on either side. During training, they would dunk us three times. The scenarios included the following:

1. The first dunk, each participant exits out the window he or she is sitting next to.
2. The second dunk, both participants exit out the left window.
3. The third dunk, both participants exit out the right window.

Jim said it was super simple. All you had to do was place your right hand on the windowpane at the bottom, unbuckle with your left hand, and swim out. If you got scared, you'd put your hands on your forehead and be pulled to the surface.

That was it. The pep talk took all of ten minutes. I looked at my boss. He looked back. I began to nervously sweat. I snapped to attention when Jim pointed to the dated boxed television playing a twenty-minute video about three dudes who work offshore. It appeared to be made in the early eighties. The video simulated a helicopter going down and what to do if we were ever in this particular plight.

The narrator's first suggestion was to remain calm and take a deep breath. Sounded about right. He then walked us through Jim's simulation descriptions. All three guys made it out safely. Hurray!

Next up? How do you respond when the process doesn't go as planned? Such as:

What if your window doesn't pop open?
What if there's a perished colleague in your way?
What if your seat belt doesn't unfasten?

Yeah, Jim. What do we do then?

The overhead lights came on, and Jim asked if we had questions. We all sat in solemn silence. He clapped his hands and said, "Now let's get out there and pass this test!"

I was baffled. We had been in the classroom for less than an hour. And we were going to the simulator? Already? Didn't I need more instruction? *Could I please watch that video again? I was distracted before by the perished colleague's mullet.* My body began to shake for fear of, once again, looking like a scared fool in front of my boss.

Jim was halfway out the door.

My nerves melted a bit when I saw a normal swimming pool with an iron cage at the end. This was it? No murky water? No dark simulator? *Oh, look! There's Jimbo! He's rockin' some sweet back hair. I guess there won't be five guys in scuba gear ready to save me. It's Jim in a Speedo. It can't be that bad.*

Our first part of training was jumping off diving boards and swimming in long lines, hanging on to each other with our legs. I made sure not to swim by my boss during this portion of the exercise. My legs were wrapped around a nice marine biologist. We practiced treading water in a circle to keep the middle guy warm. This happened to be our photographer, Mark. That wasn't awkward at all.

We had to pair off for the scary simulator part. Bill chose me. Or he was stuck with me. I can't remember the team-picking details.

We hopped into the simulator. I had been feeling a little less pukey, but then it was time to buckle my shoulder harness and lap belt. That's when I began to ponder, *Is this necessary? I mean, I'm pretty sure I'm going to perish if I go down in a helicopter. I'm okay with that. Knowing my luck, a shark will probably eat me if I happen to survive impact, get out of the seat, find a window, open a window, and swim to the surface. Maybe I should reevaluate this career path. I could write for a living. Maybe I could call ABC and see if they would give me a job as* The Bachelor's *Chris Harrison's stylist or something. Heck. I'll wait tables. Maybe go back to Disney World . . .*

That's when Jim commanded us to take a deep breath before plunging us sideways into the water. All I can remember is up became down and right became left. And lots of bubbles.

I felt for my windowpane, unbuckled quickly, waited for the suggested eight seconds to become oriented with my surroundings, and swam to the top, which felt like the opposite direction I should be going. Fresh air never tasted so good!

Back in the simulator for round two, I asked Bill if he wanted to exit my window or his window. He didn't answer. He was mentally preparing himself for the quest. I had to nudge him into reality. He decided to follow me out my window for round two. We gave Jimbo the thumbs-up sign and crashed into the water a second time.

I found my windowpane, unbuckled myself, and suddenly felt a severe push on my side. Bill was forcing me out the window! Being a rule-follower, I was waiting for the eight-second orientation phase, but in his world you survive by any means necessary. I headed out the window just as he grabbed my leg. Not for dear life, but an aggressive grab nonetheless. I basically pulled my leg through the window and he followed, popping up out of the water before me. Then he lectured me on how I need to be quicker when evacuating an upside-down helicopter simulator in the middle of a pool on the Texas A&M campus in Galveston.

After being dunked for round three, I hung around upside down for a while, making sure to give Bill some time to unbuckle and pass through his window before I followed him. I reached over and he was gone.

The dude left me to perish below.

I crossed hand over hand to escape. I'm sad to report that one of my toe thumbs became wedged somehow between two pieces of metal. With no time to waste, I jerked it out with all my might. When I reached the surface, Bill was having a lively conversation with Mark.

As we made our way to the car, we confessed to each other that we had been nervous for the first dunk, but we didn't want to tell anyone. Then we called everyone we knew to report we were alive and the training was over. Welcome to Rio!

Fun fact: The Brazil trip was canceled.

10

Livin' La Vida Loca

Another one of my overseas adventures began on a remote runway near Hobby Airport in Houston. I was traveling to Mexico with clients because I had an important job no one else in the world could be trusted to do.

They needed me to run the PowerPoint.

It took about twenty minutes for me to figure out that, when you travel via charter plane, you park in an unmarked lot and walk into a discreet miniterminal. I attempted a look of confidence to project the notion that I fly charters all the time. I tossed my bag onto a leather sofa and began to stare out the big windows, looking for my tail number.

Don't I sound smart? When you charter a plane, you have no flight number. Of course, I didn't know this bit of important information when I was first told I would be traveling to Villa Hermosa with the president and vice president of my client's company. I sounded extremely adept when I called the lady who booked my flight to gently remind her she had forgotten to provide me with a flight number. She sweetly explained the tail number rule and suggested I look for other members in my party and copy what they do.

She wasn't being mean. Oh no. This lady was the most wonderful woman in the world. When booking our plane, she had to submit passport information and the weights of all who would be on board Tail #1361SPN. She had me marked down at 105 pounds, as though I was an average sophomore in high school trying out for the drill team.

Isn't that darling? Since this was a life-and-death situation, however, and not a carnival guessing game, I was forced to tell the truth. My true weight was disclosed and an appropriate amount of "No way!" was exchanged back and forth via email.

Precious.

I spotted my tail number and tried to maintain a composure that conveyed I was a professional, when honestly, I was having trouble keeping it together. It was the smallest plane I'd ever seen in my entire life. I fought the urge to immediately text family members and friends to share my love and promise to one day see them in heaven. Instead, I wrote that I thought my seat would be in the pilot's lap because I was unsure how five people were going to fit into this tiny flying contraption.

Like Chandler Bing, I'm highly sarcastic and use inappropriate humor when I'm nervous.

My two companions arrived and went straight outside. Following their lead, I hurried out behind them and paused as they handed their bags, which were to be stored in the underbelly of the plane, to the copilot.

Decision time. I knew I was supposed to do what normal charterflying people do, but I couldn't give up what I considered a carry-on. I would rather look like that peculiar guy in *Office Space* who loves his red stapler than dig around in my bag to remove the candy corn I planned on eating and the latest Harry Potter book I planned on reading. I smiled at the uniformed man and made a beeline for the steps.

Unlike in *Pretty Woman*, there was no red carpet.

Unlike anyone in *Pretty Woman*, I hit my head hoisting myself inside the death machine.

What I wasn't expecting was to fall into a lovely, white, cushy sofa. As I tried to pretend I always crawled onto my charter flights on all fours, I slid onto the comfy couch and marveled that, somehow, the Regent Beverly Wilshire had been miniaturized and stuffed into this tiny little plane. I shut my gaping trap and buckled in for the two-hour flight.

Let the record show that flying does not bother me. But flying in quarters so close you can lean forward and smell that the pilot had garlic bread for lunch is a bit on the disconcerting side.

We arrived in Villa Hermosa at roughly eight thirty in the evening. I successfully disembarked without any embarrassing mishaps. As soon as I straightened up from descending the steps, every mosquito within a five-mile radius attacked my ankles, neck, and arms.

Interesting tidbit about Lincee: babies, cats, and mosquitoes love her.

I kept swatting the little bloodsuckers, making tiny screeching noises, when I realized three armed soldiers were looking at me as though I had lost my mind. One had a German shepherd. Where was this kind of security back home?

I calmed down, pretended to be a poised businesswoman, and let Cujo sniff my bag, willing him not to discover my candy corn stash. He didn't.

We made our way inside, had our passports stamped, and drove to the hotel. A conference room was set up so the American team members could go over the superimportant PowerPoint presentation with the Mexican team members.

I was told the president of my client's company would have his laptop. He did not. Once I swallowed my heart back down to my chest, I borrowed the vice president's computer and settled in for a long evening.

In a brilliant move, my Mexican counterpart set up his computer right beside me. We opened version sixteen of the never-ending presentation we had been working on for weeks and dutifully listened as the company president made more changes. My counterpart edited his Spanish version as I made tweaks in my English version.

You've probably never experienced the onset of a heart attack unless you're solely responsible for a dual presentation in two languages. Fun times for me.

Around eleven o'clock, the president decided the show was too long and he cut more than half the slides. This seemingly good development created a lot of work for me, especially when the vice president asked for his computer back. *¡Ay, caramba!*

I tracked down my translator friend, who was more than happy to let me confiscate his computer for the evening. I hauled it to my hotel room, turned on the lights, and for the second time that day I was captivated by my surroundings.

I was in a suite with a den, a bedroom, and a bathroom the size of my first apartment. This bathroom had robes, slippers, an Olympic-sized Jacuzzi tub, and a walk-in shower I could have Jazzercised in if slipping on complimentary Crabtree & Evelyn body wash hadn't been a likely possibility.

While listening to the Spanish version of *High School Musical* drift through the television speakers, I opened my translator's laptop around midnight to a terrifying message: *Bienvenidos* Microsoft Vista!

Not once did I anticipate that his computer would be Spanish-speaking.

For the next thirty minutes, I worked to figure out how to save, cut, copy, and paste. Vista was another roadblock. Furthermore, I couldn't figure out how to "save as" on this machine. My solution was to leave the document open all night long.

That's when the electricity went off.

I sat there in the dark, remnants of "We're All in This Together" in *español* ricocheting in my head. I grabbed my phone, and by the glow of my Blackberry, I padded around in my Hilton slippers and robe, praying for the lights to come back on. I contemplated taking a bath in the glorious tub, but I figured the jets wouldn't work if the electricity was off.

Then I thought of something equally smart: If I was supposed to drink only bottled water and it was common knowledge that you needed to keep your mouth closed while taking a shower in Mexico, what were the hygienological odds that submerging oneself into an Olympic-sized tub full of that water would result in a condition more significant than a yeast infection?

I'm going to go out on a limb and say the odds are pretty high.

The lights eventually came back on and I finished my work at three in the morning. Thank goodness for the PowerPoint girl, am I right? After washing my hair and body, I did a few deep leg lunges in the huge shower and then retired to the bedroom for a nap. I had to be up in three hours, and because I'm a paranoid freak, I kept the lights on in case I overslept through my bedside alarm, wake-up call, and phone alert.

The next morning we met again in the conference room and went through the revised presentation in both English and Spanish. Once the president was satisfied with our work, we loaded onto a bus and caravanned over to the client's offices an hour away.

To get into the building, I had to give blood and urine samples before promising to relinquish my firstborn child. I unwillingly left my driver's license with a total stranger and was ushered to a fancy boardroom to set up. The Spanish presentation was on the left, English on the right. I was prepared to do my part and help "wow" a roomful of ten to fifteen men with nothing but the power of my pointer finger.

The presentation was immaculate. Everyone loved it. Or should I say, the one dude who showed up loved it. All those bells and whistles and the hoop jumping impressed Eduardo, the drilling manager. Would he ever know how much time I spent on this presentation? Would my clients? That advance button can't push itself, you know.

Our team of seven recovered our driver's licenses and headed to a well-known high-dollar seafood restaurant for lunch before we boarded our flying Ritz Carlton later that evening.

I love seafood about as much as I love green beans.

The First Course

Take shrimp cocktail and puree it in a blender. Then heat it until it's boiling and pour it into a juice glass. Add a dollop of mayonnaise. Enjoy!

I thought I was going to gag. My plan was to daintily drink a sip from the culinary catastrophe before casually dumping it onto my plate or into a bowl while no one was looking. Sadly, this was the appetizer and there was literally nothing else on the table besides salt and pepper shakers. We sat there chugging our boiling shrimp cocktail blends, politely wiping our mayonnaise mustaches with our napkins.

The Second Course

Oysters soaked in lemon juice served in a shot glass. Kill. Me. Now.

I couldn't do it. I was still trying to control gag reflexes from the shrimp disaster. Luckily, my laptop buddy noticed the adorable shade of grayish-green my face had turned, slid his empty shot glass in front of me, and slammed mine back with a devil-may-care attitude. Chivalry is not dead. At least not in Villa Hermosa, Mexico.

The Third Course

Waiter: *"Ensalada?"*
Me: *"Si! Ensalada!"*

Yeah. Mexican salad apparently is a mixture of diced beets, bell pepper, and onion. Why didn't I sneak some candy corn into my purse? Come on, Lincee! Rookie mistake.

The Fourth Course

A lady rolled a serving cart up to our table, presenting a lovely variety of soups that were not labeled. This absence of information did not seem to bother anyone but me. Incontestably, the smartest move was to go with the cream-based selection. The others were watery, displaying a filmy grease layer on the top. I had no way to know what that woman would ladle up from the depths of that ginormous pot. Yes. Cream-based was the smart choice. I thought of it as a big bowl of queso. There were chunks of something in there, but I could swallow them down without tasting.

Celebrate the small victories in life, people.

The remaining courses were served every two or three minutes. Plates of fish, oysters, shrimp, and "salads" passed among eager eaters at our table. I chose items that were yellow or white. I also ate the same piece of bread for twenty minutes. I did have a few pieces of sea bass, a fish that swims around in the Mexican water I'm not supposed to drink.

Back on the plane, my co-travelers quickly drifted off to sleep with their bellies full of a smorgasbord of items that surely gave them the runs later. Neither thanked me for going above and beyond the call of duty the night before. Fortunately, I didn't expect any accolades.

In their eyes, I was a secretary who wielded a mighty PowerPoint. Nothing more.

On the bright side, I did get a stamp in my passport and had the opportunity to travel in style. Additionally, given that our plane was the size of a standard Buick, I started snooping through the drawers and found an entire stash of Wheat Thins and M&Ms.

That drawer is what real dreams are made of.

11

That Time I Didn't Shower
for Three Days

Toward the end of my oil and gas career, I felt I had pretty much seen and done it all.

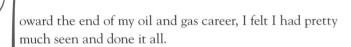

- I was held in the back room of a Colombian airport because local authorities thought I was smuggling in pirated DVDs.
- I once was lifted off a boat onto an offshore rig by a crane holding what is accurately described as a "man basket."
- I had a disturbing conversation about tattoos with a guy named Short Rib. I'm sad to report that, upon a cursory

> glance of Short Rib's various tattoos, I could confirm one was misspelled.
>
> — While on a rig in Dubai, I had to pull my hair up into my hard hat and was told by my handler, "Never leave my side. Not for a minute. These guys haven't been around a nice-looking lady in a few months."
>
> — I've heard curse words and seen girly posters that would make your mama blush so hard she could sell leftover rouge at the Macy's cosmetic counter.
>
> — And then there was the time I was asked to leave a meeting because what the men were about to discuss would probably "be above your pretty little head."

Working in a man's world can be tough, especially when these three words are introduced to your vocabulary: Alaskan man camp.

It's exactly what you're envisioning. A camp, full of men, in Alaska. Typically, man camps are set up in remote locations when logistics dictate that shuttling people back and forth to a hotel proves to be too expensive or time consuming. It makes more sense to build small dormitories wherever the drilling is taking place.

I rolled up to this particular Alaskan man camp after an eight-hour flight. A man named Tom greeted me in the dining hall and introduced me to all the guys in the room. My smile was met with uninterested grunts and apathetic head nods. We ate dinner and discussed the agenda.

Around my third yawn, Tom realized I was exhausted. He escorted me to a guy named Mikey, who was the keeper of the dorm assignments. Only one of the rooms had a door lock. The reasoning was a mixture of safety concerns, fire hazards, and the frequency with which room keys were lost. Not to mention that these guys worked two weeks on and two weeks off. Even though a legitimate system was in place to keep sleeping arrangements quasi organized, the truth was most of the men slept wherever there was an empty bed.

Luckily, Mikey assigned me the room with a lock. It also had a bathroom. I walked down the hall, stuck the key in the lock, and twisted. Nothing happened. I looked at Mikey, who was truly concerned that I didn't know how to reverse the effects of a locked door. He came over, finagled with it for a few seconds, and then gave up. The new owner of the room I was borrowing for three nights had evidently changed the lock without telling him.

Take two.

Mikey apologized for the inconvenience. I tried to be cool with sleeping in a room without a locked door. He assured me I would be safe before instructing me to take the first room on the right. I walked in, heard snoring from the depths of a comforter, and walked right back out to Mikey.

He apologized again. He meant the first room on his right. My left.

Take three.

Thankfully, this room was unoccupied. I rolled my suitcase in and dumped my backpack on the bed. I organized my coveralls, hard hat, steel-toe boots, gloves, safety goggles, notebook, and camera for the next day's activities. I was rifling through my bag looking for my toothbrush when it dawned on me I didn't know where the ladies' restroom was.

Mikey was happy to point me in the general vicinity of the restroom. I followed his directions and landed in a large, tiled area with locker room–style showers. The faucets hung from the ceiling. There were no walls. Urinals, yes. Stalls, yes. Doors on those stalls? Nope.

I kicked myself for failing to pack a modest bathing suit and privacy curtain along with a towel, washcloth, and shower cap. How could I be so forgetful?

A conundrum like I had never encountered in this business was staring me in the face. Committing to not bathing for the next seventy-two hours was an easy decision to make. I have no problem rolling deodorant over my entire body. Not using the facilities was another story. It annoyed me that there wasn't one restroom in this entire camp with an actual door.

I'll spare you the details of my lavatory schedule. After years of secretly desiring the chance to be seen on the same playing field as a man in this business, I was desperate to go unnoticed. Heaven help me if some burly roughneck came wandering through the bathroom with a towel wrapped around his waist as I hovered over a toilet bowl.

By day three I was a hot mess. Not only was I sleeping with one eye open, but eighteen hours of Alaskan daylight was definitely jacking with my brain. Linda arrived that afternoon from Anchorage so we could finalize my newsletter stories. I erratically tried to explain why I looked crazed, smelled worse, and how I dreamt about hot showers. She immediately ushered me to the private bathroom next to the dining hall designated for handicapped guests.

I cried tears of joy, thanked her profusely, and suggested she find a new position for Mikey.

My oil and gas career not only thickened my skin, but it afforded me the freedom to experience life outside of the United States. For nine years Bill let me gallivant around the world seeing new and exciting things. He also sent me to places like Bakersfield, California, where I rode in a truck with a man who didn't speak to me once for three hours, and Williston, North Dakota, where our rig directions included "turn right at the tree with a tire hanging from a branch." This East Texas girl thought it was all glamorous.

I grew a lot during those years in the oil field. I quickly figured out how to carry myself with confidence, despite being ignored by some of the good old boys. I accepted that I would be eating weird foods, and I worked hard to stretch my writing to be both informative and entertaining. Through all the Offshore Technology Conferences and rig-ups, I kept writing about music, movies, TV, Jesus, and *The Bachelor*'s Our Host Chris Harrison's amazing blue eyes on my personal website.

The day *Entertainment Weekly* reached out, I knew this side writing gig was no longer a hobby.

12

Tell Your Story

The label "academic perfectionist" remained with me in college and reared its manic head in Dr. Bishop's writing class several times my senior year. Dr. Bishop was an older, quiet man who was respected by many in the journalism department. Rumor had it he was especially good at his job, and I was lucky to have secured a spot in his class. But his syllabus was extremely fluid and lacked structure. I was rattled by the missing information from our assignments. This rule-follower needed specific rules.

Our class was small; only ten of us sat around the table that first day when Dr. Bishop asked us to write a piece that responded to the prompt, "Tell me about yourself." One guy asked if we had any parameters. Dr. Bishop shook his head no. I asked if there was a word count. He shook his head no. Another student asked if he could give us any direction whatsoever. He smiled and walked out the door.

The next time we met, he called each of us to the front of the room to read our paper. The extrovert in me was ready to perform—until the fifth student finished reading her story. I had woefully taken this assignment in an entirely different direction than half the people in the class. Self-doubt set in and Introvert Lincee tried with all her might to slowly slide underneath the table.

Dr. Bishop called my name. I walked up to the front of the class, holding my paper with shaking hands. Instead of reporting simple logistics, like where I was born or where I went to high school, I recited the following:

He has opened and closed the family restaurant every day since I was five years old. When he isn't at home, he's there. He manages employees, food orders, bills, and the countless details of what it takes to own your own business. He does this so we can enjoy full lives. His hands are strong and his mind is sharp. I am hardworking because my father is hardworking.

She has more energy in her tiny finger than most have in their entire body. She teaches, cooks, cleans, and has a habit of constantly serving others no matter what the cost. She does this so we can thrive in a happy home. Her laugh is contagious and her hair is immaculate. I am compassionate because my mother is compassionate.

She used to time me to see how long it would take for me to get her a drink from downstairs. She lets me sleep in her bed when I'm scared. She is determined and full of courage. Her talent is endless and her willingness to stand up for me when I am not feeling my best is appreciated. I feel safe because my sister is always by my side.

I like big hair and bright colors. I can recite every line from *Dirty Dancing*. I prefer Han Solo over Luke Skywalker. I know how to moonwalk. MTV and Pac-Man are my jam. I am a child of the eighties.

They laughed at me and pointed. They made me embarrassed and giggled when I cried. They eventually stoked a fire inside me that made me brave and bold. I'm a stronger person because they told me I could not do it.

He believed in magic. He didn't flinch when people told him it couldn't be done. He constantly pushed limits and envelopes. He thought outside of every box. He used a ton of pixie dust to create a place full of magic. I am a dreamer because Walt Disney taught me how to dream.

He was the Word who became flesh. He is the subject of the greatest story ever told. He walked on this earth, took on the sins of the world, and died a cruel death on the cross. He rose so that I may enjoy an intimate relationship with Him. I love Jesus because He first loved me.

Dr. Bishop asked me to stay after class. I knew what was coming, and I apologized for botching the assignment in such a huge way. He interrupted me and said he would fail me if I didn't continue to follow my gut on each and every assignment for the rest of the semester, no matter how abstractly I interpreted the prompt.

So you're giving me an A then?

Dr. Bishop was also my career counselor. The day I told him I didn't want to write for a newspaper or magazine, that I wanted to work at Walt Disney World for a living, was probably the day he turned in his resignation. Instead of helping me land an internship at the *New Yorker*, Dr. Bishop helped me land an interview with the Disney College Program.

The interviewer said one sentence to me. Guess what it was.

"Tell me about yourself."

I found out the August after graduation that I had been accepted into the program. I did little writing while at Disney World, except when I completed coursework that contributed to my Ducktorate degree.

That's right. I received my Ducktorate from Disney University. It's hanging on my wall right beside my Baylor diploma. I swear that piece of paper is responsible for all the job interviews I was offered after returning to Texas. It got me in the door for the Cowboys interview (shun) and my first real job at the Levenson Public Relations firm in Dallas. My position at LPR was more event-driven. At this point, my creative writing skills were a little rusty. I needed to shake off the dust.

I found solace in the form of a little show on ABC called *The Bachelor*.

My high school friend Julie and I were roommates at the time and unintentionally clicked on *The Bachelor* the night season one debuted in March 2002. We were hooked, but we kept that circumstantial evidence on the down low. No one needed to know we wasted our time on such nonsense. Besides, what were the odds of this train wreck securing a second season?

This is why I'm not a television producer. I don't have the vision.

A year later I was in Georgia for an event, irritated that prep work for a lavish party the next day was moving at a glacial speed. Didn't these people know *The Bachelor* was about to come on? We were well into Andrew Firestone's season, and I was invested in all the contestants. I was working with a bunch of cool girls from Atlanta, and I casually asked them if they wanted to come to my hotel room to watch the show. Just like that, three more ladies became a part of Bachelor Nation.

The next week I emailed the girls a little synopsis of Monday night's episode. My message was well received. Words of affirmation are my love language, and these women were filling my bucket.

The week after that, I was the one who received an email from the girls. They wanted to know when to expect the recap. I quickly busted one out, copied a few of my own friends, and waited for the accolades to start pouring in. What I didn't expect was an email from a girl named Tiffany a few days later, asking if she could be added to my original recap distribution list. She was bummed that she didn't get the recap until Thursday.

Hold the phone. Who is Tiffany and how did she get my email address?

A quick scan of the thread produced my answer. My friends had been forwarding the recap to their friends. Within the month, I had one hundred email addresses counting on me to report my Firestone findings. In 2006, when the distribution number hit several thousand, my Levenson IT friend stepped in. The recap had officially grown into a venture too big for me to handle via emails, so he instructed me to create a blog.

A . . . *what now?*

After a bit of research, I discovered a blog is sort of like an online journal. As much as I admired the thought of posting online like a real-live Doogie Howser, I knew I didn't have the patience to code algorithms and whatnot. I did not do technology. Cell phones were used for emergencies only in the early 2000s, and I'm not sure if laptop computers had even been invented yet. I whined until my IT guy reached the point of exasperation and walked me through the steps.

Lo and behold, blogs were just like PowerPoint! Click here for title. Click here for body. Click here to publish. I was an official techno maven.

In August 2008 I launched iHateGreenBeans as a place to tell my story. You won't be able to find those earlier posts. I accidentally deleted them, and I still cry to this day if I think about it too long.

Words are my life. Writing comes easily to me, yet I can't seem to convey how my website has affected me in ways I could never imagine. Hear me when I say it has nothing to do with the mechanics or stories. It has *everything* to do with the people on the other side of the screen who take time out of their day to read what I put out there on a weekly basis.

This thought is absolutely overwhelming to me.

I love my website. I love that I can share whatever I'm feeling. I love that it started out as a silly place for friends to come read about *The Bachelor*. With all the joy it brings, I find it completely ironic that it was born in such a tumultuous time in my life.

God took something so ridiculous and made it into something so great.

Fast-forward five and a half years. It was a complete surprise when *Entertainment Weekly* came knocking on my virtual door to ask if I would recap television shows for them. Exactly zero arm twisting was required in this decision.

I was completely willing to watch TV for a living.

For the first time in my life, I realized what people meant when they said they loved their jobs. It's not that I hated my other jobs; I just had this new perspective that I was doing what I was born to do.

My *Entertainment Weekly* editor invited me to contribute to a section of the website called The Community. We were a band of individuals who devoted our spare time to writing about television shows we enjoyed. Our piece of digital real estate had one job description: fill in the gaps.

Entertainment Weekly has staff members dedicated to writing recaps for the top television shows. According to ratings, roughly twenty-five channels have at least one hit series. Combine that with the addition of streaming outlets, such as Hulu, Netflix, and Amazon Prime, and suddenly their writing bench wasn't that deep. That's where the Community came in. Our posts provided readers twice as many recaps to scroll through.

Recaps serve one of two purposes. You either read one because you love the show and want to know how fellow fans interpreted the episode, or you read the recap because you missed the episode and need trusted input to decide if watching is worth your time.

After EW staffers were assigned their shows for the main site, a secondary list was given to Community editors. They dropped the selections into the body of a mass email and sat back as we volleyed for our favorite shows with the tenacity of women fighting Black Friday crowds at Walmart for one of those blankets that looks like a mermaid's tail.

Fortunately, my DVR was full of teenybopper shows most women my age didn't watch. Contrary to my own popular belief, no one was dying to get their hands on *Hart of Dixie*. Obviously, they had never seen the character Wade Kinsella without one of his flannel shirts. I had my first assignment. I also had a tight deadline.

As a general rule I was given one hour to complete a thirty-minute sitcom recap and two hours to finish my recap for an hour-long drama. Some networks provide advance screeners, or even an entire season's worth of episodes you can watch on your own schedule. This gives the writers the luxury of taking their sweet time to compile a well-thought-out body of work.

In the three years I've worked for *Entertainment Weekly*, I've written more than 350 recaps. Of those 350 recaps, five were written from screeners.

I don't mind the weekly deadline. I like the acid reflux that accompanies the adrenaline I feel when I'm racing against the clock. It's part of the job. The website must be updated with the latest, greatest pop culture information, and it can't be done if I don't contribute my part.

I hyperventilated after I posted my first *Hart of Dixie* write-up. And the second. I wanted them to be well received. They were. I wrote all sorts of recaps and fun evergreen stories for the Community for about a year before I was called up to the big leagues.

The main site—or the Mothership, as I like to call it—needed a recapper for *Glee*. Fox had announced it was the final season, and *Entertainment Weekly* editors thought theater kids, theatrical adults, and that significant demographic of Gleeks who vowed to stay until the final curtain call would cause a surge in ratings. Also, the show was on Friday nights and no one on staff wanted to write about a bunch of kids who wanted nothing more than a night on the town in New York City when they could go outside and have an actual night on the town in New York City.

I was personally recruited for the job after neglecting to tell my editors I had given up on Rachel and Mr. Schuester ages ago. I accepted the Wednesday before the Friday debut of *Glee*'s sixth season and binge watched seasons four and five in forty-eight hours. As I soaked in the material, I took generous notes and my head flooded with ideas and snarky one-liners. I struggled with the deadline because I wanted my first Mothership recap to be perfect. I asked my editor for a thirty-minute extension. He gave it to me since he, too, didn't have anything better to do on a Friday night than to wait for some dork to triple check her grammar and spelling.

The next day my editor told me my *Glee* recap had the highest click count, not for the week or month, but for the entire year. I know half of that milestone was a direct result of Gleeks, but the other half had to be my stellar writing. I proudly rode that high for a few days—until I read the comments.

Most of the commenters simply talked about the show and shared favorite lines from my post. A handful hated me. I tried hard to ignore them, but my brain tends to overlook the positive and overanalyze the negative. The bad stuff is easier for me to believe.

We live in a distracted world full of impatient people who are conditioned to take advantage of the instant access some platforms provide. Social media allows anyone with an account the ability to react and respond to what they just experienced.

I'd been told there would be "trolls" in the comment section and I shouldn't engage. But I did, and the ugly comments stripped away at my confidence. I didn't feel up to the task. Not only was I being cyberbullied, but my numbers tumbled down each week. I had fallen dramatically from my high horse.

Several friends encouraged me to resist finding my worth in a site demographic. I didn't listen. I checked that number religiously, multiple times a day. I had severe anxiety. This recap was becoming a full-on addiction.

Three months in, my editor announced we were switching to a new web software. The first time I logged in to the new system, the little site demographic icon was nowhere to be found. I had no way to check my daily stats because I had not been granted that privilege. Ah, detox.

Being powerless to know if anyone is reading the recap you poured your heart and soul into is freeing. The anxiety melted away, and I wisely decided to never again visit the comment section. I continued to write for both the Community and the Mothership four nights a week. I also started writing book reviews for the Associated Press and was hired to create scripts for an online show on CBS.com. They all found me through my website.

Suddenly my freelance writing gigs were filling all the extra space in my calendar. I wrote for my oil and gas clients during the workday and was tethered to my television nights and weekends when I wasn't traveling.

Around that time I read a verse in 2 Kings that said Hezekiah went to the temple of the Lord and spread a letter out before God. That's how I felt about my life. All these wonderful opportunities were spread out before me. I had to choose to jump into the unfamiliar, unstable freelance world completely, or stick with a dependable job in the oil and gas industry.

I'd like to say I confidently dove headfirst into the world of full-time writing, but honestly, I slowly sank into my new reality, fighting fear the entire way.

I continue to be a peculiar mixture of a scared, excited, giddy, relieved, tired, anxious, fulfilled, adrenaline-induced version of myself. But I have the desire to make it work no matter what. I have friends who have promised to lift me up in my times of "What did I just do?" These are the same friends who have promised I can sleep on their couch should I become homeless.

As I bow my head, humbled by the fact that the Lord has put me in a unique position to tell my story, I know He has prepared me for this adventure.

Let the new chapter begin.

it must have
been love

Is this what having butterflies inside you feels
like? Or is this the Frito pie I had for lunch?

13

They Lived Happily Ever After

Do you remember the game MASH we used to play in junior high? This highly accurate pastime could predict the future. When you answered a few questions and threw out a random number, a simple piece of paper could, among other things, tell you if you were going to live in a Mansion, Apartment, Shack, or House. According to my MASH results from seventh grade, my future self would live in a shack in Nashville with three children, drive a Jeep Wrangler, and marry Jason Bateman. In reality I lived in an apartment in Dallas, drove a black Camry, and married my high school sweetheart.

The first time I saw him was random. He stood a few doors down from me, and his calculator managed to drop from the dark corners of his locker, where I later learned his immaculately covered textbooks resided. The crash caused me to look in his direction. He nodded and smirked at his clumsiness. For some reason his gorgeous blue eyes and adorable smile had a weird effect on my insides.

Years later he told me he dropped his calculator on purpose. He wanted my attention. I never bought into that story, but it sure is more enchanting than the truth. We became friends in Spanish class. Conjugating verbs has never been so much fun as it was my senior year in high school.

I sat in the front row because that's where those of us who are fixated on maintaining a 3.8 grade point average sit. He sat in the back with a rowdy group of football buddies. Mrs. Robinson asked me to tutor the team since they were having trouble *habla*-ing *español*. This idea terrified me to no end. Me? Teaching boys what "*Donde está el baño*" means?

No thank you.

Yet there I was, in his house, holding flash cards like an adorable nerd. I was fascinated by his younger brothers walking around in their boxer shorts, eating cereal straight from the box. His mom's laid-back personality made me feel welcome whenever I visited. His dad insisted on changing the oil in my car or putting air in the tires. I always felt at ease within those walls. I relaxed and settled into my own skin, knowing these people would be cool with Freak Lincee, Bilingual Lincee, Bubbly Lincee, or Self-Conscious Lincee, who refused to swim in their pool unless it was dark outside.

This guy could have been an Abercrombie & Fitch model. You expect me to traipse around in a swimsuit in the light of day while he has all of that going on? Hard pass. I'll be over here eating the emergency Tupperware container of green beans my mother snuck into my purse before I left the house.

When I think back to those days, I remember smiling and laughing more than I ever had before. We sang in his truck (okay, I sang in his truck), and we held hands in movie theaters. He even let me paint his face as the Ultimate Warrior from WWF Wrestling one time. We tried to synchronize our after-school work schedules, and we stole glances when we drifted by each other in the hallway.

We also texted. It was called "passing notes back and forth" in the olden days.

I was a year older and proudly robbed that cradle when I asked him to be my date for the senior prom. We officially defined the relationship around that same time, and no matter how hard I tried to push it away, reality dictated that I would be going off to college in the fall. Leaving him was unnaturally hard for me. But these are the steps you must take to become a civilized, well-educated adult. At least that's what my sister told me.

I drove the three hours to Baylor University and bawled along with one of George Strait's more poignant songs the entire way. I crossed my heart and vowed to give all I had to making both our dreams come true. I knew that in all the world, my boyfriend would never find a love quite as true as mine.

My first year at college was a hard transition. Ironically, I thought Waco, Texas, was a big city, because unlike Hallsville, this town had more than one stoplight. I had to get used to the common congestion of five thousand students fighting for twelve parking spots near Packard Physics. I also pumped my own gas for the first time. There was no Tommy at the Gulf station downtown to do it for me.

I took full advantage of my meal plan and all the amenities campus dining had to offer. I was a fanatic about upholding my strict diet of macaroni and cheese, bagels, chocolate pudding, and Cap'n Crunch with crunchberries. Green beans were no longer on my radar. My freshman fifteen escalated to a freshman twenty-five once I discovered Taco Cabana served tortillas and queso twenty-four hours a day, seven days a week.

As expected, another gaggle of mean girls entered my world and made life miserable. They rolled their eyes when my daddy moved all my stuff into the dorm using a horse trailer, and they laughed at me for not knowing Harold's was a clothing store and not some guy they met in Penland Hall. I was a hillbilly loser the entire fall semester—until they found out my cousin was secretary of Pi Beta

Phi sorority. Suddenly, not only was I invited to have coffee at Common Grounds, but I was offered the front seat of the BMW on the drive there.

I passed on their invitations because I felt uncomfortable around such upscale trendiness. I called a pashmina a thick scarf, for crying out loud. What would we ever talk about? I doubt this elite group cared that I knew where the quieter spots in the library were. What would I have to contribute during an emergency squad meeting to try to figure out how to be invited to the Sigma Chi Derby Days or SAE Jungle Party?

I had a boyfriend in another town. I wasn't interested in fraternizing with any Baylor guys. I had never even attended a fraternity function.

Until I met Jill.

Before we Jungle Cruise skippers were close enough to pluck each other's chin hairs as adult women, Jill and I met during Pi Beta Phi pledge week in 1995. I knew we were meant to be together forever when she easily executed a dazzling toe touch without stretching. She also had an adult-sized Annie costume, including the wig. Not only did I need to borrow those red curls immediately, but it was evident that she and I were the undisputed choice to be elected the creative geniuses who would lead our sorority to victory at the upcoming All-University Sing.

Sing is a long-standing tradition at Baylor. Student organizations perform seven-minute Broadway-style song-and-dance numbers in competition with one another. You can see why I was drawn to this ceremonial ritual like a tap-dancing moth to a theatrical flame.

Phi Kappa Chi excelled at Sing. They typically placed every year, and Jill and I quickly became friends with their Sing chairs. Since we could dance, we were courted exactly two times that semester to attend Phi Chi functions. I like to imagine we livened up those parties with impeccable charm and jazz hands. We showed up to the first social gathering in matching ice-blue fringe dresses with long clip-on ponytails and diamond tiaras, although the event clearly called for ladies to wear sensible cocktail dresses.

Whoops.

One time a Phi Chi in our environmental studies class insisted we join him at their annual pajama party. I'm sure they were expecting us to arrive in clothing a little more risqué than button-up flannel tops with matching bottoms and house shoes.

I can't speak for Jill, but I was never invited to another fraternity party.

I was okay with ditching Date Dashes and skipping mixers, because my heart was always with my boyfriend, who lived far away. Once he moved to Austin to attend the University of Texas, we burned up Interstate 35, visiting each other on weekends. I'll admit that my time at Baylor was fun, but I lived a somewhat distracted life.

I wanted to be with him. It's all I had ever wanted, and I felt as though something was missing when we weren't together. I knew the angst Tom Cruise's character felt at the end of *Jerry Maguire*. He completed me.

For those of you who were born in the late eighties or early nineties, this was like how Jacob in the Twilight series describes the wolves imprinting on their future brides. I felt anchored and secure in his presence. Gravity was no longer holding me to the ground. He was.

Hey, millennials: he was totes adorbs #bae #truluv

We dated an entire decade. For ten years we stayed committed to each other through college and in the early stages of our careers as we settled in the big city of Dallas. We were there for each other during the ups and downs. We celebrated milestones, comforted one another during trying times, and agreed to be each other's person. This man was my world. He was strong, compassionate, hardworking, talented, incredibly handsome, and admired by so many, even though he was a Texas Longhorn. I was elated when he asked me to be his bride over a bed of roses and heart-shaped cookies.

A diamond in the middle of a sugary dessert? This man was my soul mate.

We were married in 2002. The day was hectic because of rain. I remember being overwhelmed with joy. I had my three-hundred-dollar dress, a borrowed veil, dancing shoes, and several hundred friends and family members surrounding me. That's how small towns roll when you're related to almost everyone within the city limits. The entire population is invited to the shindig for fear of hurting feelings. Heaven forbid someone would read about it in the paper's gossip column the next weekend and realize they weren't included on the guest list.

It was perfect.

The flowers were astoundingly beautiful. It was dusk, and the sun was shining through the stained-glass windows at the church, casting a magical glow on the dark wooden pews. Candles danced and the worship music brought me to tears. Then the organ swelled with an earth-shattering version of "Here Comes the Bride" as I glided down the aisle, envisioning myself as a country version of Princess Di.

My father placed me on the arm of the man with whom I would spend the rest of my life. His would be the face I saw when I woke up each morning. His would be the cheek I kissed at the end of every day. This was the man God so graciously provided to be my helpmate, companion, husband, and friend. We vowed to love each other until death parted us, and we were linked by the powerful bonds of marriage with a simple, yet boldly proclaimed, "I do."

Suddenly all was right with the world.

The reception was a blast. Mama and I somehow managed to talk my father into having the party at our house. Daddy burned every piece of wood and mowed every blade of grass in the days leading up to the grand event. My sister's husband, Gary, strung twinkling lights in trees and inside the tented driveway. The rain even stopped an hour before the blowout. The cake was scrumptious, the booze was disguised in red Solo cups, Mama didn't care that the dog's muddy paw prints were all over the front of my dress, and Daddy fried up a ton of catfish out by the pond with a big ole smile on his face.

Daddy does not smile. This was the real deal.

The photographer that night captured me staring at my husband with this look of awe. I know the feeling well. I remember constantly thinking, *How did I get so lucky? Why did he choose me? Will I ever be able to show him how grateful I am that we get to spend the rest of our lives together?*

I certainly tried. Being a people pleaser and an approval addict has its advantages in a marriage. I simply agreed to everything. I never wanted to rock the boat, except that one time I insisted on purchasing a plastic Christmas tree because I can't keep a real one alive. No one wants to wake up on December 25 to a bare-branched crispy tree with brown needles scattered all over the floor, right?

Other than that one instance, I stuck to the status quo. I cooked (read: microwaved), cleaned, and continued to excel in my career as he did the same. We lived in a tiny little apartment on the outskirts of downtown Dallas, complete with brand-new china we wouldn't unpack until we moved into a grown-up rental house in an adult neighborhood one year later.

We had red, white, and blue appliances, cookware, and linens, and way too many tin stars in our Texas-themed kitchen. He insisted we decorate with raw wood, iron, leather, and stone before it was all the rage. He was the Chip to my Joanna. The backyard was an oasis, thanks to his commitment to cultivating a tidy landscape.

I loved this man more than anything in the world. We had this marriage thing down. We had the calligraphed sign that read "They Lived Happily Ever After" to prove it. It swung merrily on a doorknob. I clearly remember the day we started talking about kids. That middle bedroom facing east was the perfect size for a future nursery. We would have one blond-haired girl, four blue-eyed boys, and one of them would definitely be named Austin. Don't worry—no one would be named Waco, Hallsville, or Dallas. The boys would wear little cowboy hats and Wranglers as my dad drove them around on his John Deere tractor. Mama would teach the girl to bake, play dress-up, and would never ever serve her green beans.

I thanked God for putting this perfect man in my life. I thanked Panasonic for making such a durable calculator. I thanked my lucky tin stars each morning that he chose me to be his one and only.

Record scratch. Turns out I was not his one. And I was not his only.

14

For Better or For Worse

I lost a receipt from a business lunch, but I needed to be reimbursed. My work colleague told me all I had to do was look online at my bank statement, print out the transaction, and turn it in to the accounting department.

Since my husband was in charge of our money, I never had a reason to visit our bank's website. After creating a username and clever password (I hate green beans), it was done! I was now a high-tech online account holder. As I scrolled through the seemingly endless list of grocery store visits, gas station transactions, and the occasional Chili's splurge, the name of a luxury hotel stopped me in my tracks. I caught my breath. For a hot second, a grim thought flashed in my head. I shook it away and chastised myself for entertaining the idea, even for a second, that my sweet, penny-pinching husband had gone to a fancy hotel with someone else.

But there it was. Taunting me from the backlit screen. The Crescent Hotel was the crown jewel of downtown Dallas. Did I mention Chili's was our splurge?

And then the answer floated into my brain like a drifting feather: our second wedding anniversary was coming up. That had to be it. He must have put a deposit down on an event room. Of course he was throwing me a party, and I had inadvertently ruined the entire surprise.

Truth be told, my insides knew he was too frugal to plan anything at the swankiest hotel in the Metroplex. He openly mocked the pretentious people who spent their hard-earned money on ostentatious places like that. I tried to focus on work, but there was a foreboding, tingling sensation rippling through my body.

After lunch I caved. I called the hotel's front desk. I explained to John the Business Manager that my credit card had been hacked. I could hear John's smirk through the phone. He all but openly guffawed at me. Biz Manager John assured me the transaction was legit and asked for my fax number so he could send me a copy.

John had evidently handled this type of call before.

The familiar scrawl was my husband's. I picked up my keys, left my entire purse for some reason, and walked out of the building holding the fax. I drove to his office, or so it would seem, because the next thing I knew I was entering the bullpen-style setup where he worked. Greetings from familiar coworkers and friends seemed to come from far, far away. My legs were moving but my ears were ringing. Apparently the sound of my name caused my beloved to turn around and catch a glimpse of my face. One look, and he knew. He escorted me right back out the door to a more private location, outside. The first words out of his mouth were, "It was only one time."

No one told me the traditional gift for a second-year anniversary had been changed from cotton to complete and total devastation.

My surroundings went sort of dark as I sank to the ground in a crouched position. Then I uttered a strange, guttural sound I have described as a deep lament of anguish that mimics a whale during mating season. I actually fell over, my knees hitting the concrete in the middle of a smoking court. Ironically, I happened to have this life-altering moment just outside the building where my husband's mistress worked. I retreated to the sanctuary of my car soon after that electrifying display of bewilderment.

He followed me home, promising when we got there to never be unfaithful again. *It was only one time. It was only one time.* He repeated this phrase as if it were his get-out-of-jail-free card. But the phrase he thought held the key for him cut me to the core. It was an admission. A confirmation of that foreboding heat that struck my gut when I saw our bank statement in black and white.

Fuzzy places and flat-out blank spots dot my memory of those first few days of knowledge. I do remember that when I finally wanted to talk about it, that phrase came back as a way to shut me down. *It was only one time.*

In other words, *Get over it.*

I swallowed my intuition and chose to believe him. I grabbed on to the "for better or for worse" part of our vows. I was staring "worse" in the face, but I would not give up on our marriage. Or our red, white, and blue kitchen, one girl and four boys happily ever after. Divorce was not an option. What doesn't kill you makes you stronger, right? I kept the affair a secret for several months, trusting that God was using John the Business Manager's fax to refine our partnership.

That December an opportunity arose for my husband to work at his dream job back in East Texas. A Christmas miracle! We could have a fresh start in the comfort of our hometown. God was affording us the opportunity to move back to our friends, our families, and most importantly, to the place we fell in love. Dallas held dangerous secrets and worse memories. I eagerly packed up the house, quit my PR job, and watched as the Crescent Hotel, the mistress, and the Metroplex shrank and then disappeared in the rearview mirror of the truck.

Like those five pounds during drill team tryouts, Dallas came back to haunt me.

In fact, it had never gone away. My husband had been leading a double life. On Christmas Day I stumbled across an email that confirmed the nagging feeling I kept pushing down. Sick, afraid, and terribly lonely, I had to let someone in on my pain. My sister had always been the brave one, so I turned to her to make me feel safe again. I told her I was confused and scared. I gave her the play-by-play of my discovery. I held nothing back. I cried as I confessed my fear of what my future held.

She had witnessed me falling in love with him. Now she was witnessing me falling apart. She said something I will never forget in the form of a simple question: "Are you 100 percent sure you're supposed to leave?"

My answer was technically no, but I was about 99 percent ready to throw in the "'til death do us part" towel. She took my hand and cried with me. Jamie knew if any tiny shred of me was still in this relationship, I had to go back to him. Otherwise I would always wonder if I could have done anything else to save my marriage and my red, white, and blue kitchen.

I worked hard to be a loving wife with a forgiving heart. I drifted around for another month, refusing to give up. But I wasn't myself. My spark was gone. Since I didn't have a job, I made it my personal responsibility to check his cell phone and truck odometer. I didn't recognize this obsessive person who was a nervous wreck, walking around on eggshells, desperate for my parents or friends to discover that I was unsuccessfully navigating a deep, dark, personal chasm.

Mama was convinced my weight loss was from green beans. I let her believe that.

The one shining light was my website. Every Monday I wrote a *Bachelor* recap and sat at my screen as sweet commenters showered me with praise or engaging questions. The community I found there quite literally helped me get out of bed. I had purpose. I didn't care if my purpose was to report who would forgo their individual room keys for the "fantasy suite" episodes. The website was like oxygen. The readers were my support system. Together they were my lifeline.

My husband didn't fight for us. I don't remember an apology. We were strangers living together. There was no laughter, just a lot of crying on my part. Our eye contact communicated different emotions than it had before. My best friend was slowly disappearing more and more every day.

I was on my knees praying for the Lord to deliver true reconciliation, yet my husband was emotionally absent. I vividly recall telling the Lord (that's right, I *told* Him) He was going to have to hit me over the head with a frying pan if He wanted me to leave this man. I begged Him to intervene.

Help me to discern.

Help me to endure.

Help me to function.

Jesus. Help me.

One cold, early January morning, I heard his cell phone ring while he was out of the room. Someone left a message. The number was from Dallas. I took the phone to him and asked what we were doing. He looked exhausted and completely miserable. The time had come for brutal honesty.

It must have been before sunrise because the living room was dark. I was in my favorite tattered bathrobe. He had just showered. He smelled clean and manly. I always preferred the fragrance of soap rather than the musky aroma of store-bought colognes. He stood in front of me with his hands on my shoulders. I remember he squeezed them a bit, probably so my brain would comprehend the words about to come out of his mouth.

He explained that what he and I had was great on paper. What he had with her was real. He had tried to leave her, but he simply couldn't.

He wanted to begin a new life with her.

Huh. I didn't remember him repeating, "I promise to develop feelings for another woman and hide it from you for six months" during our sacred vows in front of our family, friends, and every resident of Hallsville. I'll have to double-check the VHS tape to make sure, but I imagine I would recall that.

I was dumbfounded. After the truth sank in, I made a grand gesture of grabbing my clothes out of the closet and dramatically throwing them into the open mouth of the one suitcase we owned. He stared at me. I snatched the "They Lived Happily Ever After" sign and smashed it onto the hardwood floor. Then I fetched a broom to sweep up my mess.

Suddenly the frying pan hit me.

He didn't want to mend our marriage. He didn't want reconciliation at all. I chose to surrender right then and there. I called my sister to come get me and watched as my husband of two years and boyfriend of ten walked out of my life forever. The man who held my heart was heading out our front door, leaving me a cracked shell of the person I used to be.

Jamie sent Mama, who arrived in full force. She blew through the kitchen door ready to collect her daughter. I noticed her face was strong and full of sadness. I was holding two dish towels. A red one was in my left hand and a navy-blue one was in my right. I kept looking back and forth, disoriented by my new reality.

Which dish towel should I take? Do I want my future kitchen to be red or blue? What if I want it to be yellow? Do I leave them both or should I pack both? What am I supposed to do with my wedding ring? I'm not sure if I take my favorite frame with our engagement picture or leave the photograph here to be forgotten in this house that never once felt like home. Now back to these dish towels. Which one? Red or blue?

Mama caught me as I slowly slid down the kitchen wall. She held me and rocked me, wiping tears away with a fluffy navy-blue dish towel with embroidered Texas flags, knowing our lives were about to radically change.

I felt lost without my other half beside me. I was totally confused. Had I picked the wrong guy? I questioned if I knew the true meaning of love. What had I done wrong? What could I have done differently?

I had not chosen this. I believed that because I was a good and faithful person who abided by the law, served others well, and attended church on a regular basis, I should be rewarded for not being a hoodlum. I thrived best when provided a detailed rulebook.

Thou shall not steal. *Okay.*

Thou shall not kill. *No problem.*

Wait eight seconds before you exit the simulator. *Great.*

Always ask for a locked door at an Alaskan man camp. *Noted.*

Never take a water pill on an empty stomach. *Check.*

I had followed the rule in every rulebook so far. But mainly I had not been the one who broke the seventh commandment. So why was I the one suffering? Why was I the one being rocked by her mother on the floor of a rental house, clutching a navy-blue dish towel left over from her perfect life?

I could literally do nothing to stop this from happening. I had no choice but to face this new normal. Unfortunately, this unfamiliar road was full of heartache. In the midst of my divorce, I lost two grandparents and turned thirty years old. I had no job, no house, no husband. I did have two thousand dollars to my name and a car full of clothes as I rolled up to Johnny and Linea's house to move back home.

I was the juiciest gossip Hallsville had heard in years.

Papers were served. My cousin Stephanie was my lawyer. She took care of everything, including the bill, I assume, because I don't remember writing her a check. She told me the divorce would be simple. My husband and I didn't have kids, we owned our vehicles, the house we lived in for six weeks had been a rental, and I took very few of our shared possessions other than a comfy chair and ottoman that had belonged to his grandfather. They were red-and-white gingham and I adored them. And for some odd reason, I felt deeply attached to the washer and dryer. I'm also proud to report that I finally made a decision and went with the red dish towels.

Two months later, Jill drove in from Houston to support me during D-Day, as we called it. Stephanie wore a sensible suit, Jill wore something darling, I'm sure, and they both talked me into putting on pants and brushing my hair that morning. We walked into the Gregg County Courthouse three years and 214 days after I pledged in front of God, my family, and all of Hallsville to have and to hold the man whose name was now at the top of a piece of paper. A plea of irreconcilable differences in front of the judge and one slam of a gavel later, and I was officially allowed to dig out that box of stuff in Mama and Daddy's attic that had my old monogram on it.

I stood there stunned. I was legally ripped away from someone I had built a life with for the last twelve years. The entire exchange took thirty seconds.

And just like that, I was Lincee Leigh Ray again.

Jill insisted we go back to my parents' house to dine on queso and pink lemonade daiquiris. Mama gave us the stink eye. The clock read nine thirty in the morning, but she couldn't come up with a solid defense to divert our attention from Ro*Tel cheese dip and rum once I played the "I just got divorced" card.

Jill invited me to join her in Houston for a few days. We made a pit stop at her mom's house on the way. When we walked through the front door, her mom, Pam, and her prayer ladies rallied around me as Kelly Clarkson's "Since You've Been Gone" boomed from the sound system. They cheered for me as I walked through the victory line with big tears streaming down my face.

We weren't celebrating the end of my marriage as a victory. We were accepting the authentic truth that it was time to move on. We were rejoicing that I could breathe normally for the first time in months. These women knew I had a long road ahead of me and that signing the papers was the first step out of a deep hole.

I knew I was being refined. I faced each new hurdle with as much grace and dignity as I could muster. I thanked God for this thorn. I worked on understanding that His power is made perfect in my weakness. I knew I had to keep telling myself these truths, even though I didn't believe any of them.

It was the worst time of my life. I was a mirage of Lincee. Although I technically stayed away from fully flinging myself into the abyss, I did peek over the edge a few times. I have never experienced pain, rejection, emptiness, and hopelessness like I did in those months. Holding it together became my full-time job. I longed for the weight to be lifted off my chest. Darkness had settled in. I felt lost, weak, depressed, unloved, invisible, ugly, and forgotten. Just to name a few.

One night I couldn't sleep. I was pacing around the familiar contours of my childhood bedroom. I bumped into memories of my husband everywhere. A stuffed animal he gave me on one of our dozen Valentine's Days looked at me with dead eyes. I could faintly make out a burnt-orange Texas hat hanging in the closet. Folded scraps of notebook paper littered the room with his familiar handwriting, "For your eyes only" heralding one of a million love notes High School Lincee had saved. Our wedding picture now held a prominent place in this little girl's room.

The clincher was the snapshot from the prom date that started it all. I stared at the innocent girl smiling in the frame, knowing how her story ended. I ached for her. I ached for us. I ached for me. This was torture. I began to hyperventilate, and with the onset of a panic attack approaching, I sat down on the floor and put my head between my legs. With the paraphernalia of my past surrounding me, I cried out to the Lord with my entire being.

Where are you, God? I am a good person. You call me your child and you are just going to leave me here in all this pain? I can't pray anymore. I can no longer put one foot in front of the other. Obviously, this is the life you have planned for me, and I think it sucks. What did I ever do to deserve this? I have nothing else to say. I have nothing else to give. I am done!

After my temper tantrum, I confessed to the Lord that I didn't know what to do, what to pray, or how to be. I calmly surrendered everything by admitting that I couldn't fix the emptiness. I knew I had to move on. I wanted to move on. I placed all my burdens at His feet.

And that's where I really met Jesus. At the crossroads of my life, I looked to His cross.

This time, a nail-scarred hand held me tightly by the shoulders and said, "I know what it's like to be rejected. Don't be afraid. You are not alone. I see you and *I* will never leave you."

15

A Little Help from My Friends

The mirror was the first place rejection took me. After my divorce, I became skilled at analyzing my appearance, concluding that my husband left because I hadn't been pretty enough. He'd probably wanted someone younger with longer legs. The good news was I had lost ten pounds on the divorce diet without even trying. The bad news was I figured I needed to lose about twenty more pounds to even be in the realm of "hot status." I assumed his hotel gal was a *Sports Illustrated* swimsuit model, and that I needed to lift and squeeze parts of my body for anyone to notice me now.

Does Botox hurt?

Then I wondered if he left because I wasn't smart enough. I must not have challenged him on an intellectual level. Maybe he finally realized I have an awkward personality. Or I'm too sarcastic. Perhaps he found me uninteresting. I should have read more *National Geographic* magazines while studying for an advanced degree.

Then the dreaded "you're too nice" moniker hit me like a ton of bricks. What if he wanted more give and take in our marriage?

A confident wife who stood up for what she believed in. Was I a doormat?

Finally I landed on a blanket statement of what I considered to be truth at the time: *I'm not good enough for him, and he figured that out.*

When I added up the looks, the weight, lack of intelligence, sarcasm, and nine other items on the rejection list, I rationalized that I was unlovable. I also refused to accept the reality that sometimes good people suffer.

I was a joy to be around.

My grandmother tried her best to encourage me. Mimi talked about how a man named Job lost his family, home, health, and financial stability all at once. Standing over the ten fresh graves of his children, Job cried and said, "The LORD gave, and the LORD has taken away; blessed be the name of the LORD" (Job 1:21 NKJV).

I decided to dig a little deeper into this Old Testament story. I bought a book by Charles Swindoll shrewdly titled *Job*. If anyone knew why good people suffer, it would be this biblical figure.

Job taught me to hold everything loosely. God gave Satan a permission slip to wreak havoc on Job's life, and Job responded with grace. He did cry out in confusion (been there) and question his position (done that), but he never cursed the name of God.

The ending royally irritated me, though. I'm not talking about the part where God restored everything Job lost at the beginning of the book. I'm talking about the part where we never get an explanation for why Job had to suffer in the first place. Job asked, "Why me?" several times in forty-two chapters and never got an answer. I needed a formula.

When would God give me a detailed description for how to get through tough times like his servant Job did? I knew because God is sovereign I was supposed to be cool with whatever he had planned for me, but I wasn't there.

Why did my ex get to be remarried while I was left alone? Why did his new wife look like a supermodel while I was worrying about all my insecurities? Where had I gone wrong? What could I have done differently? How was this fair? I was standing in the epicenter of pain, disappointment, and frustration, and God expected me to say, "Blessed be the name of the Lord" for my trials?

Yes. Yes, He did. And He does.

In moments like these, you can do one of two things. You can wallow, or you can pull yourself up by your bootstraps and move on.

Dear readers, I wallowed. I wallowed big time. We're talking gummy bears and Cheetos in bed while watching *Friends* reruns and a good solid two weeks without a shower. No less than eighty-four people informed me that "This too shall pass." Others emphasized that infidelity was a two-way street. They wanted to know what I had done to make my husband's head turn after another woman.

After I honestly deliberated punching each one of them in the throat, I fought to be patient like Job, resting in the hope that my life would one day be restored too. Slowly but surely that hope began to push its way back into my life as the months dragged on.

It started with my people. The women in my life who understand the importance of a good cry and a much-needed scream. These women know when to be silent, but they can also quite literally pull you out of the fetal position. These are your steel magnolias. These are the ones you want in the trenches with you.

My trenchmates are mighty. God blessed me with incredibly strong women who know Him and can speak truth into my life. One of these women is Jill and another is our friend we met at Baylor named Rebecca. I honestly don't know where I would be if they hadn't broken through the stale haze one day when I was holed up in my old trundle bed, reeking of cheese dust and regret.

Mama and Jamie did their best to invite me back into the land of the living, but I wasn't having it. I preferred to be horizontal, thankyouverymuch. I wanted my surroundings to be dark and cold as I rocked back and forth murmuring the lyrics to "Smelly Cat" under my breath.

One day Mama crept into my room and handed me the phone. It was Rebecca. I valued our talks because Rebecca had been down my road. She knew what I was feeling. I remember asking her how long it was going to take before I felt normal again. She anticipated that it would be five years. I hung up on her.

I successfully dodged calls from my cousin/attorney, Stephanie, and our college roommate, Caroline, as well as from Julie. I was becoming one with my pajamas, and I didn't need any of these shiny, happy people pretending to know what I was going through.

Weeks later, Rebecca called again and I answered. She had a challenge for me. All I had to do was get out of bed and put on my shoes. When I asked her why I had to put on shoes, she had a logical answer: if I had shoes on, I wouldn't get back in the bed. Rebecca granted me extra perks. I didn't have to put on a bra or makeup or do my hair. I only needed to be vertical and modeling some sort of footwear.

I could do that. Of course, I puttered around my room all day, but I was standing. Victory.

Jill tag-teamed the next day. She called and had a new challenge. All I had to do was get out of bed, put on my shoes, and then go outside. I remember protesting. If I was going outside, did that mean I had to wear a bra? I was astounded to learn Jill didn't care if I wore a bra. The goal was fresh air. If I walked outside for a few minutes, the day would be credited as another victory.

So I did. I inched out of my cocoon, and with great caution I re-entered the world.

I'm pretty sure Mama burned my bedsheets. Or she repurposed them as outdoor pillowcases for pool lounging. Regardless, she and my sister were relieved to see me trying to put my life back together.

The most liberating truth someone once told me is that it's okay to feel what you feel. It's natural to acknowledge you feel frustrated and misled by where God has you in life. It's not as though He doesn't already know you feel that way.

This truth gave me the freedom to stop brooding in my own personal darkness. I finally faced my new reality with fresh eyes. I was no longer afraid of other people seeing me as weak. I ditched the fake smile for earnest eyes and asked myself legitimate questions:

Who is Lincee Ray?

How am I going to make a living?

Where do I go from here?

In the middle of a time when I had no idea what I was going to do, I decided to focus on what I did know.

God is good. It says so in the Bible.

Trials will come. It says so in the Bible.

He's got this. It says so on my screensaver.

I get it now.

The Lord has given and the Lord has taken away. Blessed be the name of the Lord.

At the end of the day,

If the *only* reason I met the man of my dreams

If the *only* reason I reveled in the glories of marriage

If the *only* reason I fought the anguish of adultery

If the *only* reason I endured the sorrow of divorce

If the *only* reason I mourned not having a child

If the *only* reason I immersed myself in a blanket of depression

If the *only* reason all of this happened was to put me on my knees every single day in communion with my Lord because I didn't know what else to do or where else to turn . . .

Then praise be to God.

mother may i?

Eat your Twinkie and report back to me if anyone
is bleeding. That's my childrearing motto.

16

Cowboy Ken

I played with Barbies until I was in sixth grade.

Phew! It's good to admit that out loud. I've been carrying it around for a while.

Oh, and it wasn't one or two Barbies. I had sixty-three. More than half were hand-me-downs or wonky ones my grandmother purchased for a dime at Canton Trade Days. Yes, Peaches-N-Cream was my favorite. Thank you for asking. And yes, each one had a name. You can stop judging me now.

When I was five years old, we moved from a trailer house into a brand-new home my parents still live in today. Mama purposely put two closets in my room so I would have a place for my Barbies where they and all their paraphernalia could be hidden away. Little did she know my Barbies liked to go on road trips.

The architect built the closet like any other. It included a bar to hang long dresses, two bars for shorter skirts or tops, and two sets of stacked shelves on either side for shoes and accessories. Barbie's Knock-Off Dreamhouse fit perfectly under the tall bar. Luckily, the pull-string elevator was right next to the first set of stacked shelves. How else would Barbie's friends get to their individual apartments?

I designated the other shelves as garage space for Barbie's silver Corvette, Ken's Jeep, the horse trailer, and the sixties-style van that once belonged to my older cousin. The bottom shelf was the stable for the horses. It was a happy coincidence that Mama covered all the floors in the entire house with hunter-green carpet. It made sense for the horses to graze on this level, because the carpet was an obvious substitute for grass.

I spent hours in that closet. I'm sure my parents felt relieved that I had taken a break from belting out the latest show tune at the top of my lungs, wearing a feather boa and a green felt hat, to draw on Barbie's sizable family tree, including spouses, children, and pets.

In short, I loved my Barbies.

I remember the afternoon I decided it was time to pack them away. A friend had turned up her nose upon the discovery that I still played with dolls, and I made the decision to move on and grow up. I was twelve. I knew I was too old to be taking Barbie on adventures every weekend, but part of me hated the idea of closing the closet door on this chapter of my childhood. I cried as I boxed them up.

To this day the Barbies are still in that box at the top of my closet in my parents' house. I couldn't stand the thought of them going in the attic. It seemed more humane to keep them where I could see them. And where they could breathe, obviously.

One day I went home for a visit and saw my Cowboy Ken lying on the cedar chest at the end of the bed in my room. Mama had expertly selected him as a prop for Vacation Bible School that summer. She glued cotton to his face for a beard and sewed him a tunic. My beloved doll had been morphed into Joseph with an amazing technicolor dreamcoat. The sight of the glue that undoubtedly scarred Cowboy Ken's face for life literally brought tears to my eyes.

I was thirty-six years old.

Crying over a defaced Barbie as an adult proves I am indeed an emotional person, but those tears I cried over Cowboy Ken surprised me. Why was I so upset? Truth be told, I had two Cowboy Ken dolls. If anyone ever played with them, Joseph could be the other Ken's crazy twin brother who only came around during family reunions every other year. What was my deal?

Then it hit me. The tears were more than an expressive response to the multiple uses of Gorilla Glue. The startling reaction came from a place of mourning. I was grieving my desire to one day have a little girl of my own to carry on my legacy of playing countless hours with Barbie, stretching her imagination and molding her creative mind. My plan to fall in love, marry again, and have children of my own suddenly seemed far-fetched.

In fact, it seemed downright unrealistic.

For as long as I can remember, I have wanted to be a mother. With my experience bringing up Barbie's extensive family, I'm confident I'd be pretty good at it. I also have comprehensive knowledge in raising a Cabbage Patch Kid named Ancita Zara and one beloved Strawberry Shortcake doll.

As children of the eighties, we were taught young girls could do or be anything we wanted to be. We could have careers in law, medicine, or education. I harbored the secret that my life plan was to be domestic. I certainly wanted to go to college and have a glamorous job in a skyscraper, but that was a means to an end. Eventually I would get married to a wonderful man, have babies, and choose to stay home with the kids. I would bake cookies, buy shin guards, help practice spelling words, and tell elaborate stories about fairy princesses and noble knights.

Joseph triggered an emotion I had not yet encountered on my road to divorce recovery. There I stood beside my Barbie closet, holding an old friend, suddenly grieving the children I never had with my ex-husband. It unearthed substantial sadness that was still buried deep in my heart.

Mourning a lost future with my husband was one thing.

Mourning a family that never existed was quite another.

Anger quickly washed over me, and my sad tears became hot with rage. God blessed my ex with a wife and two kids. I was still alone, unexpectedly processing through this great feeling of inadequacy that I had not fulfilled my lifelong plan of being a mom.

This is the portion of the pity party when you might get riled up and do one of two things:

1. Wonder why I'm not having a baby on my own.

   On more than one occasion, individuals have suggested that I don't need to wait around for one of those husband fellas. They inform me women raise babies all the time without a man. Have I considered insemination? Of course, there's always adoption. Those kids need a loving home too. Many wonder if I have thought about fostering a child. My doctor once asked me if I wanted to freeze my eggs for posterity, seeing that I'm such an old dust bag. You never know . . .

   Here's the truth: I have not been called to do any of those things, so I'm not going to pursue them.

2. Mentally chastise me for not celebrating the here and now, because I have an ultrafabulous life.

   You are right. I thank God every day for the multitude of blessings I have received.

   Here's another truth: It's hard for me to rest in the reality that I am not a mother, especially when I have friends who are churning out their third and fourth kids. I often feel left behind. Or I feel excluded. Or I feel kindly sheltered from maternal talk since I have nothing real to contribute to the conversation. I go to the bad place, assuming I will never be able to experience true friendship with moms in its fullest capacity because I can't relate to motherhood.

Lies, lies, lies.

One of the many mantras that bounce around my brain on repeat is that God's timing is perfect and He is sovereign. I truly believe that statement, but some days something feels missing. It's an ache that won't go away. Typically, these agonizing days come when I'm restless and decide to check social media.

After mindlessly scrolling through Facebook one afternoon, I felt bombarded by a steady stream of status updates I longed to write on my own page. I found myself weighed down with the heaviness of wishing for a life that wasn't my own.

Natalie is pregnant!

Julie had her baby! It's a boy!

Gus is potty training!

Abby won a medal for swim team!

Andrew lost a tooth!

We loved seeing Alexandria dance in her recital!

Closing Facebook was easy. Reciting Romans 8:24–25 was easy. "In this hope we were saved. But hope that is seen is no hope at all. Who hopes for what they already have? But if we hope for what we do not yet have, we wait for it patiently."

Yeah, that patient part at the end? Not so easy for me.

Within minutes of staring at Cowboy Ken, bumming myself out because I wasn't fulfilling my self-proclaimed purpose in life of being a parent, I received a powerful email from my friend Sara that included a photo of a boy in Rwanda. He was holding a Superman T-shirt I bought for him. His name is JD. He's my sponsor kid.

Wow. He's my kid.

I traveled to Rwanda and met him the day before Thanksgiving in 2012. I have never been more nervous in my entire life. I was afraid he would be offended that the crazy white girl was pushing Jesus on him since one of my gifts was a Bible. I didn't know how

I was going to communicate. What if he stood there, uninterested in me? What if he expected more from his sponsor?

All my worries melted away when this twelve-year-old kid came crashing into my arms the second I stepped off the bus. He was as tall as I am, and I buried my face into his neck, tears streaming down my cheeks. He smelled like a boy—dirty and sweaty. I pulled away to look him over, and I was greeted with the biggest smile I'd ever seen.

He dragged me to his house, all the neighborhood kids following because they saw I was carrying a brand-new soccer ball. I can still hear the sweet ring of children's laughter. JD's enthusiasm was infectious.

When we reached his house, my heart broke for this boy. His home was a one-room mud hut with a door but no windows. It was tiny and dark. His mother had laid out a tattered strip of colorful cloth on their one bench because she knew I was coming. My translator explained she was at work and was sorry to miss me. I nodded as our team filled the room with a mattress, mosquito net, rice, cooking oil, soap, and the small goodies I'd brought from home.

I opened JD's Bible to Jeremiah 29:11 and started to read the familiar phrases:

> "For I know the plans I have for you," declares the LORD, "plans to prosper you and not to harm you, plans to give you hope and a future. Then you will call on me and come and pray to me, and I will listen to you. You will seek me and find me when you seek me with all your heart."

I needed JD to understand that even though his family and friends had every right to feel abused, forgotten, and broken, I was proud of him for being courageous, passionate, and full of joy. I needed him to know my prayer was for him to prosper and have hope in his future.

I needed him to know I saw him.

Slowly but surely, I sank into a fit of ugly crying, too overcome with all the feels to even read a single verse. I'd like to thank my translator for intervening, Holly and Ann for assuring me that melting down was entirely appropriate, Christina for silently praying for me to hold it together, and Emily for documenting the entire experience on video. It's a precious celebration I never want to forget.

Then the translator asked JD if he wanted to say anything, and he thanked God for his many blessings. I'd like to point out that the child didn't own any shoes, but he was grateful to God that his burden was light. Talk about convicting.

Then he asked when I was coming back to see him again. Heart. Ripped.

So of course I went back two years later. He was in a new house, and his mother wept as I greeted her child with the same thundering crash as years before.

Don't you love when God shows up in your life in a rather big way to remind you He's got this and you should just calm down?

Newsflash: *It's not about me.*

I had big aspirations in my life that included a house full of tiny mouths to feed, carpool karaoke, and family vacations to Disney World. Never in my wildest dreams could I have imagined I would be helping raise a Rwandan boy.

It's extremely humbling and exciting, and I can't wait to see the man he grows up to be. I can see the Facebook status updates now.

JD is in school!

JD is celebrating his birthday with a new pair of shoes!

JD is the coolest kid because of his Superman T-shirt. *I wonder if he knows who that is?*

JD is learning English!

JD says he loves me.

That last one makes me cry.

17

American Girl Games

I will never forget that day. It was a blustery sixty-five degrees in District 77005. I pulled the collar of my winter coat around my neck, thankful I was only a few miles from home. That's when the call came. Remembering, I'm transported back to that exact time and place.

"I need your help," she blurts. My sister is never one for small talk. Jamie is strong and assertive. Because she is a rock, the panic in her voice is unsettling.

"What is it?" I ask. Something tells me I need to maintain composure. I try to exhale slowly, but my breathing comes in uneven spurts. My pulse is racing.

"It's Isabelle," she says. "I can't find her."

I stop in my tracks, forcing everything inside me not to scream out in angst. I am angry with my sister for not securing Isabelle earlier in the month, yet equally afraid that our family will never speak to her again for the pain she will cause. I know the burden of acquiring Isabelle will fall on my shoulders. The dread slowly sets in, hardening my heart, as I wait for the reaping.

"You have to go get her," my sister pleads. "Addison will be crushed on Christmas morning if Isabelle isn't waiting for her under the tree."

Addison. At this time, she is the five-year-old light of my life. My niece means the world to me, and only weeks earlier, when I visited District 75650, we sat side by side, perusing the catalog. Horses, ballet bars, hair extensions, and tiny bracelets. It was all there, ready for purchase with the simple click of a button.

And Isabelle was the jewel, the treasure, the lifelike doll waiting to be plucked from the golden cornucopia.

"We're too late," she says. "We checked the website and Isabelle is no longer available. You must go in person and secure her. Please. For Addie."

Of course I will go. Like Katniss Everdeen from *The Hunger Games*, I will volunteer as tribute.

Back at home, I have so much prep work to do with so little time to do it. I research Isabelle's face, wardrobe, and accessories. I fuel up on Oreos and pigs in a blanket. I stretch and practice throwing stiff elbows, feigning an apologetic facial expression. Finally, I take out the small loan I know I will need in exchange for Isabelle.

It's a strategic move for me to wait until dusk to venture out into the wild. I figure young children will be out of harm's way, which turns out to be a correct assumption on my part. Navigating the mall parking lot is a different story. I decide to go on foot, with only a small ration of water, some Orbit gum, and a squashed granola bar in the bottom of my purse. There's no turning back now.

Maneuvering in and out of vehicles is easy. Pride is on my side as I roll my eyes at the driver of the Toyota waiting impatiently for a family of six to scramble into their minivan. Others circle the lot as if they are hungry sharks, following people walking in the opposite direction like chum. Oh how they will scream in vain when shoppers don't use keyless entry on any of the cars in the front row. Finally, I reach the edifice and psych myself up for my quest. This is what I have been training for. I am ready.

I push through the revolving door and land in a sea of historical dolls, their accompanying paperbacks, and special DVDs with bonus footage. I try to put my game face on, but I am immediately paralyzed by the sheer size of the American Girl doll store.

Where do I begin?

Is that a salon?

Who is Kit and why am I drawn to her like I am to my morning ice-cold Dr Pepper?

I rush to the wellness corner and fall into the fetal position by a doll in a wheelchair and one wearing headgear. While rocking back and forth, I state to myself what I know to be true.

My name is Lincee. I'm from District 77005. I'm here to get Isabelle.

My name is Lincee. I'm from District 77005. I'm here to get Isabelle.

The hysteria passes. I stand up and assess the situation. To my left are Bitty Babies. To my right is an actual café with Capitol children feeding imaginary food to their dolls. I decide to move forward. That's where most of the people seem to be congregating.

A woman picks through a clothes rack, looking for a size six pajama set to match the one her daughter's doll will be wearing on Christmas Eve. A small child screams in agony at the insurmountable volume of choices. A man pushes by me. It's only after he's out of sight that I hear the word *Isabelle* issue forth from his mouth.

I race after him, ready to fight or barter. I'm prepared for whichever scenario presents itself. I bust through an actual teepee and find the promised land on the other side of the makeshift prairie. An Isabelle display stands before me. The man and I both grab a box and stare each other down, unsure if we are friend or foe. He spies someone behind me and bolts.

"I see you've picked Isabelle!"

I slowly turn around to see the face behind the voice. She is young. And a little too friendly for my taste. *What does this woman want with me? Can she be trusted?* She hands me an American Girl tote for my treasure and smiles blankly in my direction.

"I'm Maggie. Are you interested in any of Isabelle's accessories?"

"Leg warmers!" I shout with a little too much enthusiasm.

Wait, what am I saying? Check the doll for wonky eyes and bendable appendages. Get in. Get out. Head for high ground. That was the plan!

"Perfect! How about a set of purple and pink tutus?"

My lip begins to twitch. I'm unsure. I stutter as Maggie begins shoving little pink American Girl boxes into my American Girl tote.

"Did you know since Isabelle is the Doll of the Year, she won't be available for much longer? Now is the time to buy all the accessories you want. Maybe you should take a look at the Isabelle starter kit."

I feel a wave of nausea wash over me. Either my bag of American Girl crap is getting heavier or my knees are buckling. I sit down on the floor to call my sister, a doll relaxing in a plastic bubble bath fortifying my uncertainty.

"They want me to buy the starter pack," I babble. "She's Doll of the Year and everything goes after this month. I don't know what to do. The leg warmers. *Isabelle needs leg warmers.* And a purple tutu, right? I'm about to eat the special berries in my pocket and end it all right now unless you tell me what to do!"

Jamie does what a smart, assertive person does. She consults the grandparents.

"We are a go for the starter kit," she answers. "I'm still betting on you, Lincee. Make this happen. And stay alive."

Maggie shoves seventeen more boxes in my American Girl tote and points me in the direction of the cash register. The attendants are quick and nimble. It's my turn, and I hoist my wares onto the counter.

"Would you like to purchase the special outfit of the day that includes a dress, shoes, and velvet headband? It's only fifteen dollars."

I look at her with cold eyes. I tell myself not to be a hero and shake my head as I hand over my credit card.

I leave the American Girl doll store with a new perspective on life. I have been to war and will live to tell the tale of Isabelle. They will write stories about my bravery.

And the day the odds were ever in my favor.

18

Lincee Poppins

I know what you're thinking. You're wondering why I wrote an entire chapter dedicated to motherhood when I'm technically not a mother. What could I possibly have to say?

Funny. My editor asked the same question.

I may not technically be a mom, but I do have a ton of surrogate children who love me unconditionally. I work hard to make sure each one of my friends' kids likes me more than the adults who provide them with food, shelter, smocked clothing, and Nickelodeon.

Parents endure a certain anxiety when figuring out how to raise future well-behaved citizens of this world. I field phone calls with questions like the following on a regular basis:

Should we go gluten-free?

What about dairy-free?

Is vegan-light a thing? Or do you have to be all the way vegan?

At what age should a kid get a cell phone?

Is Snapchat the devil's playground?

I don't remember dealing with mean girls in preschool. Did you?

Who is Lululemon and do I need to buy her a gift at the end of the year?

Is it normal to have this outlandish impulse to coldcock my child with an etiquette book?

I never have to worry about any of that stuff when I babysit. I show up at the house, have fun playing imaginary games, and demand that we eat dinner anywhere but the kitchen table. What's not to love? I refuse to charge for my services, so most of the parents let it slide when I leave them at the end of the night to deal with a mass of children crashing from a sugar high.

I show up, bring cupcakes, have fun, and leave nothing but joy and a few crumbs in my wake. It's what I do.

So you can fully experience the bond I have with the special kiddos in my life, I asked a few of my friends to share what happens during one of my babysitting shifts. Here's what they had to say.

Caroline—Childhood Friend

There was a three-month period when my husband, Michael, and I needed a place to live because our new apartment wasn't going to be available by the time our current apartment lease was up. Lincee graciously offered for us to stay with her. I assured her that our two-year-old son, Teel, would not be a bother. She was naive enough to believe me, so I jumped at the chance to incorporate an extra set of hands and free childcare into my daily life.

Within two weeks, Teel could hum the theme song from "The Young and the Restless." I can't decide if I'm horrified or proud of that reality. Had Michael and I not been a constant presence in Teel's life, Lincee would probably still be tied to a chair in that apartment to this day. She let that little boy rule the roost in a *Lord of the Flies* sort of way. I once found him walking around in his diaper, covered in butterfly and smiley face stickers he discovered in the depths of a bottom drawer in Lincee's room. There had to be at least one hundred stickers all over his body. Lincee thought he looked adorable. I thought he looked like that pole in the quad of a college campus where musicians announce their next gig and students desperate for money sell their living room furniture.

Those noteworthy stickers were from a legitimate scrapbook store, which meant the adhesive backing was the equivalent of super glue. Every time we tried to peel one back, Teel would scream his head off. We rubbed and scrubbed to no avail. We finally tried Sea Breeze (thank you, Linea) and rejoiced when the paper magically began dissolving. Sadly, the stickers left little red marks all over his skin. Even though he looked like he had leprosy for the month of November, we still loved him.

Okay, what Caroline didn't mention was that this particular madness unfolded on Halloween night and Teel was going out as Elvis Presley. And he won a costume contest, thanks to my suggestion that we present him as "the later years Elvis" due to the hives and antibacterial aroma. It was a brilliant plan that resulted in a plastic trophy I'm sure they cherish.

Jill—College Friend

The day Sam was born was a day to remember. He was my first child, my beautiful, tiny boy. Lincee was beside herself that I was all grown up and responsible for raising an actual human being. I was totally game when she suggested we celebrate this milestone with a fun photo shoot. She arrived at my house a few days later with her camera in tow, a big smile on her face, and a list of potential creative props.

Her first suggestion was to lay Sam near a watering can. In a word, it was lame.

Then she asked me if I had any intentions of planting some flowers in my backyard. I knew where she was going and wasn't comfortable placing Sam in an empty clay pot with a hibiscus taped to his head. Not only did that seem too girly, but I didn't feel like rolling up to the pediatrician's office the next day, explaining to the nurses why my week-old son had some awful rash one might contract from a fun day of gardening. Lincee also considered shoving him into a pumpkin, but it was April and we didn't have immediate access to that elusive gourd.

Her last suggestion was extremely sentimental. My father was in the final months of his fight with cancer, and Lincee thought it would be a perfect tribute to have Sam pose with Dad's old, worn-out cowboy boots. She both carefully and forcefully stuffed my sleeping baby into one dusty Lucchese and began snapping away.

I had misgivings that Sam would resort back to his in-utero ways while chilling in the boot, and sure enough, his little legs and feet curled up, causing my child to be tightly encased in handcrafted, high-quality cowhide footwear. Sam was legitimately stuck, and Lincee was unwilling to let me cut my father's boot with my good kitchen scissors to rescue him. She looked at me completely at ease and instructed me to "Go get some butter."

Whenever I smell popcorn, I think of that day.

Jill may have experienced a bit of ill will toward me for jamming her kid into a boot. I get it. But let's not forget that she also has a newborn picture of Sam framed in her home that would make Anne Geddes proud!

Julie—High School Friend

Lincee earned the nickname Slink in grade school when she won an award. The principal didn't know how to pronounce her freakishly spelled name, so she phonetically broadcasted that "Linky" Ray was student of the month. That morphed into Slinky, which was later shortened to Slink for all intents and purposes.

My entire family has called her Slink since the early nineties.

My son Barrett became fast friends with Lincee once he was old enough to understand she was a permanent fixture in his life. He also loves that she plays tractors with him on the floor and has serious conversations about the proper placement of the sheep, donkey, and baby Jesus in nativity scenes.

She also has no problem being Barrett's own personal human jungle gym. I've asked her on numerous occasions to explain to him that Aunt Slink needs a break, but she insists that the hair pulling and neck twisting do not bother her in the slightest. We have rules against horseplay during dinnertime, but Slink doesn't mind (read: encourages) roughhousing. Since she lives so far away and her visits are rare, we often allow the rules to be bent and watch as our child laughs with pure delight at something silly Slink does.

We also watch as he falls off the bench and cracks his head open, listen as he cries out in pain, and try not to flip out at all the blood. I'm sure this scary experience is teaching him an important life lesson, right?

He did learn an important life lesson. One lucky girl in Barrett's distant future is going to find him extremely attractive because scars are manly. Everyone knows this.

Rebecca—College Friend

My kids regard Hallsville, Texas, as the greatest place ever. When Lincee first invited us to visit her parents' house, I was ambivalent. I have four children. That's a lot of Pack 'n Plays, toys, potty breaks, and mouths to feed. My crew can be a bit much if you don't know what's coming. Johnny and Linea welcomed us with a blow-up mattress, fresh towels, and enough food to feed an army.

Not only were my urban children able to see a frog in its natural habitat, but I was able to sit on a back porch and watch as they ran on acres and acres of land. I didn't have stranger-danger fears or kids-running-into-the-street anxiety. It was wide open spaces surrounding a house, a barn, and one big pond.

My son Jackson was five years old when Lincee first took him fishing. Her family believes if you want to participate in this activity and you can tie your own shoelaces, you are old enough to bait your own hook. I had no idea rules like this even existed.

Lincee spent hours teaching him not only how to put a worm on a hook, but also the intricacies of taking a fish off said hook, should you be lucky enough to finally catch one. She also explained the circle of life when Jackson took several minutes to free his perch and tossed it back into the water, only to find it floating up to the top.

Jackson became proficient in the art of angling that year. Lincee set him up with a tricked-out tackle box for his birthday. He was in hog heaven. I took him to a fishing spot near our house and was disgusted when he asked me to pass him a worm from a Styrofoam box. I mustered the courage, prayed to the good Lord not to vomit, and handed my son a long, slimy, wiggling nightcrawler.

He gawked at me because Lincee said you're supposed to pinch the worm into thirds so you don't waste it. All you need is enough worm to cover the hook. I tried not to pass out as my son snapped the little guy's head off.

My bad, Rebecca.

Natalie—Church Friend

When my daughter Kate was born, Lincee informed me she wanted to be the first name on the childcare roster. Bearing in mind that she's a well-known baby whisperer, I've employed her services on many occasions. She and Kate bond over their love of Minnie Mouse and eating foods that come from boxes or resealable bags.

Once, Lincee watched as Kate ate a handful of various snacks she found discarded in the hatchback of her tricycle. I'll admit Kate is a brilliant child for discovering such a clever hiding spot. Or should I say hoarding spot? Regardless of the phase she may have been going through, there is no telling how long the morsels had been back there. Kate survived to tell the tale with minimal digestive distress.

Please do not confuse me with that mom who freaks out over a few stale goldfish, but I do draw the line at a moldy apple core. I can confidently say that if a kid asked Lincee, "Hey! What's this I found in the deep, dark backseat crevices of the car?" she would respond, "Lick it and find out!"

Lincee also taught Kate a few current dance moves at a church event. (Of course she did.) My daughter "whipped," "nae naed," and even executed a perfect stanky leg. Our family has fully embraced this distinguished piece of pop culture pie since Kate undoubtedly has talents unmatched by any ordinary two-year-old.

Just you wait, Natalie. I'm already expecting your call in sixteen years announcing that Kate received a full-ride scholarship to the urban hip-hop dance division at the Juilliard School. Oh, the places she'll go!

Catha—Church Friend

One of my favorite things about Lincee is that she shows up in times of need. The weekend my mom ended up in the hospital, she was my first call for help with my four-year-old. Truth be told, if my sister wasn't so great, I'd probably choose Lincee as Henry's guardian. She has a mother's heart.

Lincee arrived to take my son to lunch at Chick-fil-A, followed by a movie. Henry could barely process the idea of so much fun packed into one afternoon. All that was missing were a few hours of "watch me put this puzzle together" for it to be a perfect day.

When you're in emergency mode and things are chaotic, babysitting details aren't a priority. Lincee is a grown adult. She knew not to let my son run with scissors, wander off by himself, or jump off the roof of the house pretending to be Superman. I also knew she would spoil him rotten, allowing him to get some candy at the theater. I just didn't care at the time.

Hours later, we picked Henry up at the Memorial City Mall parking lot. He bounded out of Lincee's car and ran toward me with the spastic energy of a child who had devoured an entire large ICEE from the concession stand. Why is my example so specific? Because the remnants of the delicious cherry treat were not only all over his brand-new church shirt, but the slush had stained his mouth, chin, teeth, and fingers.

Lincee was extremely apologetic. She explained that she tried to hose him off in the bathroom, but the stains would not budge. Never underestimate the power of red dye. Sure, Henry had class pictures the next day, and the image of his pre-K photo will forever remind me of Bozo the Clown, but I'm glad he has that memory with Lincee. Because the next time he tastes the sweet elixir of an ICEE will be the day he drives himself to the 7-Eleven.

Wait until I introduce him to Dr Pepper. His life will be forever changed.

Stephanie—Cousin

We were fortunate enough to have Lincee join us on a family vacation a few years ago. If you ever have the chance to travel to Walt Disney World with her, I highly recommend it. She can tell you the best places to eat, when a long line isn't worth the wait, and all the shortcuts to get from here to there.

We basically followed Lincee around all day long unless touring plan strategies dictated otherwise. For example, at one point my mom and I took my younger son to meet Buzz Lightyear and Woody. Lincee invited my seven-year-old, Benjamin, to join her and my husband in the line for Tower of Terror.

Benjamin claimed to be too old for *Toy Story* character autographs and made the decision to follow Lincee. This surprised no one. He's practically her shadow. Where she goes, he goes. Even if it's to a place that has "terror" in the name. For forty-five minutes, Lincee sent me pictures of my son as they made their way up to the scary hotel. Captions read, "Wish you were here in our line!" and "We're not afraid!"

Let me assure you that Benjamin was afraid. He was deathly afraid. I could tell by his facial expressions. When we reunited, Lincee elaborately revealed how she held Benjamin's hand as a possessed elevator jolted my kid up and down and back up again before plummeting to the ground. She said he had the best time and showed me the picture to prove it.

Benjamin tackled a fear. He may never ride an elevator again, but I've always believed stairs are an excellent form of exercise. I consider this a win/win.

Jamie—Sister

My daughter Addie calls my sister Slink. I call her "dork" or "weirdo" or "hey you" when I'm feeling nostalgic.

Addie loves her Slink. I once saw Lincee ask Addie to mop up a spill on the kitchen floor and the child obeyed immediately. It's so annoying.

Lincee always one-ups me by watching countless hours of YouTube videos about Shopkins and singing along with gusto to the *Frozen* soundtrack instead of threatening insanity like a normal human being. I suspect she secretly gives Addie money or candy when I'm not looking.

I can remember only one time when Addie was not picking up what Lincee was laying down. After Addie grew out of all our old Cabbage Patch Kid doll outfits, Lincee insisted we dress my then six-month-old as one of those round shower puffs you find in the bodywash section of Walgreens.

To my knowledge, she had not recently helped a friend decorate for a *quinceañera*, so I'm not sure why my oddball sister had in her possession yards and yards of turquoise tulle. She took great care looping the material in rows all over one of Addie's onesies. She even found some thick white rope in Daddy's barn and made a string in case Addie wanted to hang from the faucet later. My daughter fought Slink the entire time she tried to coerce her into that itchy monstrosity. Instead of offering my help to wrangle the kid, I sat back and laughed.

As if that wasn't enough, Lincee put a matching tulle bow around Addie's head. Then she plopped her into the master bathroom garden tub, handed her one of my mom's decorative soaps in the shape of a seashell (which Addie immediately put into her mouth), and called for my husband, Gary, and our parents to come and see our real-life puff!

Addison lost her mind and didn't make eye contact with Slink for a solid twenty-four hours. It was the best day ever.

I'm glad Addison has Lincee in her life. My sister has a sensitive heart. She understands the desperate need to stop everything to find Barbie's missing boot or an American Girl doll's velvet hat. Lincee will also be the one to tell me the American Girl doll's name is Isabelle and she is an inspired dancer who is simply trying to find her own way to shine. I'll nod my head and take a bath while the search continues.

And I'll be there when you exit from the steam-filled bathroom with a soft blanket, a big bowl of chips and queso, and my Netflix password. And in true Ray family tradition, I'll also teach Addison a fun new game where we time her to see how long it takes for her to go and get us a drink refill.

I've never experienced morning sickness, labor pains, or the sweet relief of an epidural. I could never truly understand the sleep deprivation that accompanies newborn bundles of joy. I don't have to deal with repeating myself all day long, multiplying LEGOs, missing shoes, repeating myself all day long, little kiddos with bad aim who don't know how to flush a potty, spontaneous meltdowns in the toy aisle in Target, and repeating myself all day long.

But I'll be there for you at the hospital when that baby comes. If you need a nap, I will wrangle children. I'll happily change a diaper, build numerous fighter jets with LEGOs, help search for a missing shoe, clean the pee around your toilet, and escort your tired kid from the toy aisle so you can do what you came to do—wander aimlessly around Target holding your coffee from Starbucks. I will repeat myself all day long, because I love your kid. And I love your kid because he came from you.

From your womb to your wardrobe, what's yours is mine. This also includes fashionable accessories and any snack you may have in your purse.

relationship status

I communicated back and forth with a
guy on a digital dating site for thirty-nine
minutes. That's the longest relationship I've
had since the Clinton Administration.

19

All the Single Ladies

Picture it.

Dozens of us are masterfully working the dance floor. I soak up the energy of all the wedding guests around me, ecstatic that we have no problem celebrating the bride and groom's eternal commitment to each other by collectively agreeing that, yes, it is fun to stay at the YMCA. We "bring sexy back" with reckless abandon. Shouts are issued both a little bit softer now and a little bit louder now. Unless the deejay's next selection is "Macarena," this event is quickly going down in history as the best wedding reception ever.

Then it happens. I hear the familiar hand-clapping opening cadence of that song. A strange and primal survival skill kicks into overdrive and I realize I need to be as far away from this place as possible. I exit to the left, convinced that something or someone over there will be enthralling enough for me to pretend that he, she, or it is of critical importance. I see Amy scurrying off to the bathroom. Of course! That's the most logical place to hide.

"Oh my goodness! I love this song! *Come on, Lincee!* Dance with us!"

With any other classic dance anthem, I would comment on her effervescent spirit and high-fashion shoe selection as we sashayed onto the floor, but how could I when this endearing girl with zero gifts for recognizing blatant mortification on someone's face is dragging me to the middle of the one place in the immediate vicinity I simply do not want to be? A gaggle of twentysomethings sings each and every word with gusto. Many encourage me to join them by executing the now-famous moves that traditionally accompany this masterpiece. I oblige, pump my arms, wave my left hand in the air to the beat, and pretend to be empowered by Beyoncé's salute to all the single ladies.

Worst reception ever.

Take that experience and couple it with the age-old tradition of the bride hurling her bouquet into a sea of friends who are husbandless, and you've stumbled upon the recipe for my worst nightmare.

Wait a minute. Strike that. Me, the only female adult on the floor, standing alongside the bride's niece as a community of married people cheer for me to snatch the oncoming nosegay from the hands of an eager tween girl.

That is my worst nightmare.

My name is Lincee and I still have massive anxiety when I'm singled out for my singleness.

But God knows me. He knows my struggles. He knows my desires. He labels me His "child" and will do great things through me if I let Him. Acknowledging that He is good and His timing is perfect, I claim Exodus 14:14: "The Lord will fight for you; you need only to be still."

That simple verse gives me hope. It's a hope that one day a Jesus-loving man will like it enough to put a ring on it.

20

Lessons Learned
from *The Bachelor*

The first *Bachelor* episode I recapped was during Andrew Firestone's season. It debuted in the spring of 2003. I remember enjoying his stint as America's most eligible bachelor because he openly ridiculed the fundamentals of the show. He once approached a hot tub (shocker) and was laughing hysterically because the show runners had turned off the jets. The bubbles produced too much noise, rendering the audio useless. The audience wouldn't be able to hear the stellar conversation that was about to go down.

Firestone sat in a large tub of motionless, tepid water with a champagne flute in hand, unable to control the giggles. You could almost see the wheels in his head turning as if to say, "Is this really how it's done?"

Most people's knee-jerk reaction is to haughtily report that this is not how it's done. Steeping in one's own sweat juices while attempting to make casual conversation with a perfect stranger rocking a string bikini does not seem like a logical place to fall in love—particularly when a small camera crew films the entire tête-à-tête.

Let me be the first to admit I have no idea how this reality franchise has churned out dozens of seasons and spin-off shows, especially taking into account so few success stories. Is there a method to the madness? Why do we keep tuning in year after year?

For me, the answer is twofold. I fully admit that I enjoy gazing into Our Host Chris Harrison's intense baby blues in high definition television. To quote the great Debbie Gibson, "I get lost in his eyes. And I feel my spirits rise and soar like the wind. Is it love that I am in?"

Don't get me started on his crisp gingham shirts and impeccably tailored suits. We'd be here all day.

Additionally, I appreciate a good romance. Each season I carefully weigh the choices and root for the guy with the perfectly chiseled jaw and athletic build to get the girl with adequate hair extensions and a propensity to scrapbook. Who am I to deny their love quest? Maybe this will be the season when two crazy kids finally make it work!

Some of you are rolling your eyes at me right now. I understand. I, as a member of Bachelor Nation, am completely aware we're a special breed. Our ranks may not be as strong and plentiful as the supporters of the pumpkin spice movement, but we are a dynamic faction. Most of us fall into one of three categories:

1. On *Bachelor* show nights, we flagrantly mock our Facebook friends' status updates for watching such blatant filth, even though the episode has conveniently been playing in the background as we fold laundry.

2. We silently agree with our Facebook friends' status updates on *Bachelor* nights, but would never in a million years "like"

said status because mothers-in-law could see it and threaten to call child protective services.

3. Our Facebook status keeps a running count on how many times the words *amazing* and *journey* have been articulated during the current season.

For those of you who don't indulge in this reality mishmash, I've included a quick rundown of what goes on each week during one episode of *The Bachelor*.

About twenty-five girls are selected from a large assortment of video submissions to compete for a chance to win the heart of the bachelor. The producers remove all remnants of the outside world, fill the women with generous amounts of alcohol, and force them to live together in a big mansion.

Each week our bachelor springs one lucky girl free from the cell block and whisks her away for some alone time. As I mentioned before, these dates typically include sitting in idle hot tubs, flying in fancy helicopters, and riding in vintage automobiles up the coast. Sometimes they travel to exotic places like New Mexico, and occasionally they will attend a private concert given by whichever musical group is dropping an album that week.

Group dates take place too. The bachelor coerces the girls to compete for special one-on-one time by proving their athletic prowess, demonstrating their musical gifts, or testing their knowledge of geography.

At the end of each episode, roses are bestowed to the women with whom the bachelor has a connection. The losers are sent home after an exit interview. A fair number leave gracefully, but there is always one classy broad who spouts bitterly that life isn't fair. Mascara streams down her face as she wonders out loud, "Everyone tells me I'm a catch. If I'm so great, then why don't I have a rose?" A hired psychotherapist pats her on the head, tucks a bottle of water under her arm, and shoves her toward the driveway, where the rejection limo waits to shuttle her back to the airport.

As the weeks go on, our bachelor inevitably develops feelings for more than one contestant. One clueless girl always loses it when she witnesses "her boyfriend" making out with the skanky girl who "isn't here for the right reasons."

This is when storylines get interesting.

The day finally comes when the last woman standing waltzes up to the designated proposal area in an evening gown worthy of the Miss Texas pageant. Our bachelor pours out all his previously guarded feelings before dropping to one knee. He presents her with a one-of-a-kind engagement ring designed by Neil Lane, and they indulge in champagne toasts near a body of water at sunset, reveling in the moment when he can finally admit to the world that he loves her. Who cares that he may have also told the runner-up he loves her? This is the real deal.

In that instant, the official clock begins, counting down the approximate 180 days until they are no longer contractually obligated by ABC to be a couple. They sell their breakup saga to US Magazine, thereby extending their obligatory fifteen minutes of fame and later turn up in Vegas as the special guests of a "Single and Fabulous" party on Valentine's Day at the MGM Grand.

It's a good show.

I have been recapping *The Bachelor* for a quarter of my life. I'm going to pause now so you can marinate in that sentence for as long as it takes for that definitive detail to soak in.

Feel free to bless my heart.

Since I have been recapping *The Bachelor* for so long, I think I have become a connoisseur of how to manage the intricacies of the dating world when considering what *not* to do while courting a would-be suitor. Here is some wisdom I've gleaned from countless hours watching other people's amazing journeys to find love.

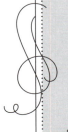

1. Research shows it takes only six seconds to make a first impression. Don't waste those six seconds singing the lyrics to a song you wrote, gifting a lame tchotchke, reciting poetry, dancing the Cha-Cha Slide, dressing like Santa Claus, or carrying an ostrich egg around. Try to be cool. And normal.

2. Do *not* purchase your shorts from Build-A-Bear.

3. Do *not* make me rebrand your denim shorts as denim panties.

4. Speaking of short, check the length of your evening gown. No one should confuse your dress with the costume Michelle Kwan wore when she won the short program in the 1998 Olympics in Nagano.

5. Do *not* drink your dinner before meeting your date. Vast amounts of alcohol lead to several unfortunate scenarios. Ugly crying. Unnecessary four-letter-word rants. That voice you hear telling you to jump in the swimming pool fully clothed? That's the gin and tonic talking. Don't do it.

6. Learn to adapt. You may have to swim with pigs when you assumed you would be swimming with dolphins. Go with the flow.

7. Never talk bad about the other women in your date's life, even if one of them made fun of your cankles. Save it for your journal, or the tell-all book deal you'll secure once you're voted off the show.

8. By no means should you present the bachelor with a jar full of memories depicting milestones in your relationship. You've only been on three dates. That's creepy.

9. If your plunging neckline is so deep it looks like your exposed sternum is being prepped for heart surgery, button up.

10. If I've said it once, I've said it a thousand times: leggings are not pants.

11. In that same vein, a shirt should not be a substitute for a dress. This is a perfect example of when leggings should be worn.

12. As for the men, ask yourself, "Could my skinny jeans be confused for leggings?" If so, stop shopping in the juniors department.

It seems easy enough, right? Make a connection. Get the rose. Have an amazing journey along the way.

Sadly, I identify more with Andrew Firestone when it comes to my dating life, especially in this day and age. Every single time a millennial introduces me to a new dating app, I sigh and marvel that this is what it has come to. I can't tell you how many times I've furrowed my brow, said a quick prayer, and expeditiously swiped right, only to be brutally rebuffed.

Until the day I tried Hinge.

21

Would You Like to Date Batman?

*P*resenting myself as an eligible lady is tricky business. I should be a well-oiled machine after watching so many seasons of *The Bachelor*. Alas, I am not. I'm more of a flailing ball of awkward who often wonders if guys still think it's fly when girls "stop by in the summer."

With the onset of online dating, one might think this would be my introvert jam since it takes the initial human contact out of the equation.

One might be wrong.

A few girlfriends and I signed up for the dating app Hinge. It's the one that connects you through people you know (or someone you know who knows you) through Facebook. I've tried all the online dating options. None have worked. I have honestly never received any sort of communication through an online dating service. I never get winky faces or likes or hearts or chats or direct messages.

Before you suggest I put myself out there and make the first move, I want you to know I have dropped my digital hankie on more than one occasion. It doesn't seem to matter. It's like a vast, empty West Texas plain in there, with tumbleweeds blowing through.

The idea of connecting with someone through the internet makes a lot of sense nowadays. The world is at our fingertips. When I have a question, I consult the Google. When I want to buy something, I ask Amazon to deliver it to me. Why shouldn't my next date come from a URL?

I'll tell you why. Because it's ridiculously bizarre, unbelievably scary, and incredibly intimidating.

Yet there I was compiling another online profile. I answered Hinge's basic questions (age, education, career, search radius) and chose from a stockpile of whimsical tags like world traveler, country clubber, dance machine, and secret agent. With one click of the submission button, I had entered another dating arena, partly basking in the hope of a romantic future and partly basking in the potential of great writing material from eccentric nutjobs.

Hinge turned out to be an eye-opening anthropological experiment. First, I was certifiably amazed by what some men chose as their leading profile picture. I tend to judge people based on this simple decision alone.

Dude, do you not have a normal picture of you standing there smiling? Because if you don't I view this as a red flag. We all have smartphones with cameras. We've all been in front of that famous landmark or that cool sporting event, surrounded by people who feel fine taking our picture because that means we are then obligated to take theirs. Additionally, if you are an incessant selfie taker, I think you either don't have any friends or you are full of yourself.

I know this makes me sound like a horrible person, and I'm trying to give people the benefit of the doubt by looking on the proverbial bright side. However, some of these guys deserve my finger's quick reaction to "swipe" them out of my digital queue. Here is a list of the more disturbing profile pictures I've received.

- The guy picking his nose.
- The guy holding a girl a little too intimately to peg her as a beloved sister.
- The guy with a Batman mask covering his face.
- The guy sitting on a toilet.
- And my personal favorite, the nipple twister.

Don't ask.

Hinge basically matches you with people in your same ZIP Code. The bonus is that it also tells you the person's name on Facebook who made this a love match in the first place. The advantage is that you can call your friend and inquire, "Is this guy a serial killer?" But more often than not your friend has no idea who you're talking about because he or she is not friends with Potential Serial Killer. Someone *they* know on Facebook is friends with Potential Serial Killer. Also, that person probably went to elementary school with PSK and hasn't seen him since 1983.

When you open Hinge, you see a long line of potential suitors from which to choose. You can either affirm them with a heart or snub them with an X. If you heart him and he hearts you, then you are deemed a match. You are whisked to a separate chat room to get to know one another better. (I suppose a disclaimer is in order. I was told this last bit of information by fellow Hingers who were slaying the system. This phenomenon had never happened to me before thanks to my tumbleweed epidemic. Hinge's internal infrastructure was a mystery to me. I knew nothing beyond hearts and slashes.)

This process got manic when Hinge introduced a new rule that was completely annoying, yet brilliant on their part. If you didn't check your Hinge every twenty-four hours, your queue was deleted. I was angsty at the discovery of this new mandate. What if I forgot to check my roster of suitors one day and my soul mate was deleted into oblivion because I was too busy doing something stupid, like working or teaching or visiting my ailing grandmother?

I'm obviously exaggerating. Hinge is green, meaning they respect the environment enough to recycle the aggregation of available men knocking down my digital door each day. If I happen to miss my soul mate, he'll probably rotate back through the system eventually. Fingers crossed for the nipple twister to cycle through again!

One day I was flipping through my Hinge suitors when an attractive guy popped up. Let's call him Isaac. He looked normal enough. His pictures described a wide range of interests. His profile was relatively safe. I decided to give him a heart.

Suddenly I got a message from Hinge that Isaac had hearted me too. *Oh happy day!* A gentleman caller! I paid attention, aware that I was about to be transitioned into the special chat room. What should I wear?

The chat room is basically your typical text message screen. The Hinge app encouraged me to begin speaking with Isaac immediately, because time was wasting. Seeing that I believe chivalry is not dead, I chose to let Isaac be the one to reach out first. He was the boy, and I needed to feel pursued even though he had already hearted me. Of course, I hearted him, too, so he basically had a green light to type with the confidence of a man who would not be rejected during this crucial initial stage.

Be bold, Isaac!

The next day I received a notification from Hinge that Isaac had typed something. I punched the app button, excited to read what interesting tidbit Isaac had to share. I got this: "Hey."

I stared at the "Hey," wondering if Isaac purposely omitted an exclamation mark so he wouldn't appear too eager. I tried not to be disappointed that our first volley of communication was a less-than-resounding "Hey," so I opted to be chill and wrote a simple "Hey" back.

It hung there, without punctuation, tormenting me. So I threw caution to the wind and wrote a smart, engaging sentence after the obligatory "Hey." And Isaac responded. We went back and forth, charming each other to bits.

As luck would have it, the special chat room allows you to see your suitor's name so you can properly cyberstalk him with the Facebook friend you have in common. I texted my friend Amy, and although she didn't personally know Isaac, she knew people who knew people who did. A cursory glance of his Facebook page led her to verify that Isaac seemed stable, right-minded, and most likely not a murderer. Sweet.

I chatted with Isaac for the next thirty minutes. He was a delight. Then the following thread transpired:

LINCEE: Who's the young lady in some of your pictures?

ISAAC: My daughter. She's a Daddy's girl.

LINCEE: I can tell!

ISAAC: She's ten. She loves to sing.

LINCEE: Please tell me you took her to the Taylor Swift concert.

ISAAC: No. That would mean I would have to go with her ;)

LINCEE: Come on Isaac! Haters gonna hate, hate, hate, hate, hate. Shake it off!

The anticipation was killing me. I couldn't wait for Isaac to respond. Similar to a regular text, I could see that the message had first been delivered, and then I saw it was labeled "read." The text bubbles were billowing, confirming that Isaac was surely writing something along the lines of, "You are so funny!"

Then the text bubbles went away. How very curious!

A two-hour meeting loomed ahead of me, so naturally I checked the app just before entering. There wasn't a notification from Hinge that Isaac had responded, but maybe Hinge was broken. Not quite. My supercreative comeback was sitting there without a response.

When I got out of the meeting, I checked the app again, only to find Isaac had deleted me.

He *deleted* me.

What in the world?

I called all my squad to tell them the disturbing news. Everyone gasped and then laughed at me. But it was my friend Ann who had the sweetest reaction of all. She automatically predicted that Isaac had accidentally deleted me. I have to admit this did cross my mind. It felt exactly like the times (yes, plural) when the boy doesn't text you back and you assume he has been in some horrific car accident. It's not as though Isaac didn't understand my humor. He had included a winky face in his previous response. You don't haphazardly throw a winky face around like it's a thumbs-up or praise hands.

Upon inspection of the app, I determined that deleting a match is a three-step process with a huge message asking, "Are you sure you want to do this?" at the end.

Applying for a loan at a bank is easier than erasing one's digital footprint from this app. No way was it an accident.

Ann was kind enough to go to the next logical theory. There must have been some sort of software error. This was a compelling concept, but if Isaac wanted to get in touch with me, he could have. Thanks to my abnormally spelled name, I am totally Googleable. I think Isaac just wasn't that into me. He couldn't handle my sarcasm and was scared off by my wit and humor. Or he truly loathes Taylor Swift and doles out winky faces to every Tom, Dick, and Harry. Or in Taylor's case, John, Jake, and Joe. If that's the case, we never would have worked out anyway.

I chose to accept this micro-connection as a small victory. I had recently prayed to the Lord, asking him to show me some sort of encouragement when it came to dating. I needed a boost. Clearly Isaac was not for me, but the experience was a thirty-nine-minute answered prayer.

I do wish Isaac well in his future endeavors on Hinge. You never know, he might find his own nipple twister in the future. I truly hope they live happily ever after.

22

This Might Not Be
an Everlasting Love

The following is a list of online dating horror stories collected from friends. I include this section in my book because I want those of you who have never experienced the nausea of online dating to know what some of us are going through. I also want my digital dating peeps to renounce their misconception that they are the only ones who get matched with weirdos.

We're all in this together, but I omitted names because this stuff is embarrassing. Enjoy!

He Did Not Just Say That

— On a first date, my match asked me, a lawyer, "What's your favorite provision of the constitution?" He proceeded to give me a pocket constitution with his favorite parts highlighted for me to read before our next date. First of all, we the people need to get a life. Second, everyone knows it's the commerce clause or no clause.

- My roommate and I were matched with the same guy. He sent us different answers to the same questions. So we sent him the exact same answers to every question.

- I was uneasy when he asked for an "action shot" of me playing soccer. Assuming he was joking, I flirted back and said, "Only if you send one first." He sent a picture of himself from high school. The illusion was shattered. We went on one date, and eight months later I saw him at church, standing next to a woman he introduced as his fiancée. Four months after that, I heard his wife was pregnant. I hope they got a really cool action shot during the delivery.

- I was matched with a friend from high school. He circumvented the awkward "no thank you" button by sending me a warning message on Facebook that he wasn't interested. #GoMustangs

- One guy's profile said he was on staff at a church. When we met for coffee, I learned he works as a checkout clerk for Lowe's. He sometimes sang with the band at church, so close enough.

- I was thrilled to be going on a date with this guy. He came and picked me up, and when he escorted me to his car, he opened the backseat door since there was another girl already sitting in the front seat. I should have called shotgun.

- Do you know about all the different types of marijuana? I do. Thanks Match.com!

- My date told me he built hovercrafts in his garage. I was tempted to take a field trip to see them just for fun. I am pretty sure he was not from the future. I know he was not a part of mine.

— I asked a guy what he did in his spare time. He said he liked to walk through the park late at night playing his guitar for strangers and the homeless. Most guys merely answer, "Hang out with friends." This guy spreads musical joy. Weird, potentially life-threatening musical joy.

— He was six feet eleven inches tall and hit his head on the ceiling of the place where we went to have drinks. He also chugged four Long Island iced teas in an hour. I offered to call the *Guinness Book of World Records* people to see if we could get him in the next year's edition.

— I went on a first date with a guy who ended up being way too interested in hypnosis and mind control games. Needless to say, he was no Jedi and we didn't go on a second date.

— A guy ordered water on our date, so I paid for my own drink. Then he suggested we go to the movies. He conveniently didn't have any money or a credit card to pay, so I did. The next week, he asked me out again. I gave him my Hulu password and told him to have fun. I'm kidding. I politely declined.

— My blind date turned down the menu a waitress tried to hand him because he was creeped out by eating in front of other people. I described each bite of my salad in great detail as he watched me enjoy my meal.

— I went on a first date with this man who told me he wanted three children. I shared with him that I wanted two. He looked me square in the eyes and informed me that we weren't going to work out since he was already mourning the third child he would never have with me. I mourned the dinner I had been looking forward to and left before appetizers were served.

I think it's safe to say most of us have been in a dating drought at one time or another. Excluding my thirty-nine-minute "wildest dreams" encounter, the most action I've seen lately has come from doctors I meet during head-to-toe medical examinations. Attempting to banter with potential future boyfriends is challenging when adrenaline is coursing through your veins. Instead of appearing elegant and magnetizing, I adopt the laugh of a giggling hyena and often break out in a nervous sweat. Although my flirt always seems to be on the fritz, I do manage to make them laugh.

23

A Scratch for Every Itch

After all that time spent on online dating apps, who knew developing a skin rash would be the key to discovering an untapped dating market?

Allow me to explain.

Johnny Ray is a tad accident prone. My dad has been bucked off horses, fallen off tractors, stung in the eyeball by a yellow jacket, and was once chased by an aggressive firecracker that whizzed up his leg. He has broken almost all his ribs, cut off his own finger, and always sports some sort of scab or oozing wound thanks to his aversion to wearing gloves. If Daddy isn't bleeding, he's probably asleep.

Based on this information, I'd like for you to try to harness the trepidation I felt when one spring day he announced he would be trimming some trees around his property. He waltzed up the driveway with his new toy in hand, yanked the box open, and produced a piece of equipment that terrified me to my bones. It was basically a Weed eater with a chain saw on the end.

This should be fun.

Once every extension cord we owned had been joined end to end, he meandered into the yard, carefully selecting his first conquest. I jogged up beside him to assess the tree. The pesky limb bothering my father was way out of reach. I suggested we start with a bush or a tree with branches closer to the ground. Hey, maybe we should read the tool's directions!

He looked at me as though I was a moron and commanded me to go fetch the ladder. Our first foray into the superfluous branch business included holding a large, top-heavy piece of cutting machinery while balancing on a ladder. Sounds about right for Johnny Ray.

Daddy handed me the trimmer while he finagled the ladder up next to the trunk of the tree. My confidence deflated when I noticed the ladder was covered in duct tape. *Lord, help us.* He scrambled up the ladder about halfway and barked for me to pass him the stick of death. I hoisted it above my head and into his open hands. Then I grabbed the ladder to support my 220-pound father, who was currently placing the tree trimmer against a limb directly above *his* head.

At this point, my sister, brother-in-law, and niece all gathered on the back porch to watch the festivities. I guarantee you they were taking bets to see who bled first. Jamie started catcalling when Daddy ascended the ladder for a second time. We repeated the same steps we'd employed for the first tree, again with zero safety precautions—except this time Daddy used so much muscle to cut a thick branch that when it finally broke, the tree trimmer swung down and around from the force. I had to jump out of the way to escape death. Gary gave me a hearty cheer for my quick reflexes.

Daddy called down, "Did I get you?"

My brain raced to that *Friends* episode when Joey drilled a hole through the wall into Chandler's room and nearly nicked his head. I reactively shouted, "No, you didn't get me! It's a tree trimmer. You get me, you kill me!"

We pruned several trees that afternoon. At one point I grabbed the branch whacker to see what all the fuss was about. I cut a few limbs and felt something. I believe they call it "power." It was glorious. When Daddy suggested I stand on the picnic table to finish the job, it made sense rather than walking all the way across the yard to get the duct-taped ladder. I was a trimming machine.

Unfortunately, that heroic experience resulted in a terribly itchy rash all over my abdomen. Please do not presume my wardrobe was to blame for this unfortunate circumstance. I did not spring break it in a bikini while chopping tree branches with my father.

Fast-forward an entire week. The skin on my abdomen was on fire. I lifted my shirt and was shocked by the raised bumps that itched like crazy. No amount of topical creams or gels alleviated the burning. I tried Epsom salt baths. I took Benadryl to attack it from the inside. I slathered myself in all the essential oils I owned. This only angered the rash. It retaliated by spreading.

Four days later, I drove to Jill's house to celebrate her birthday. I was miserable. My dermatologist couldn't see me for another week, so Jill called her doctor, who secured me an appointment for that afternoon. Jill is a redhead and she has her skin doctor on speed dial. He's practically family and will apparently do anything for his favorite ginger. I nonchalantly asked what he was like.

Jill has known me for two decades. She looked into my eyes and immediately understood the question behind the question. She offhandedly offered that he's around one hundred years old and a lovable, captivating oddball. I had nothing to worry about.

A woman's abdomen is an intimate place, in my opinion. The idea of lifting my shirt to reveal a rash that had taken up residence in the folds of my mid-region was enough to bring on the sweats. Jill knew I needed to know Dr. Davis was not going to judge me for my lack of abdominal muscles.

Jill gets me.

I drove to his office, filled out the necessary paperwork, and headed into a little exam room. The nurse was pleasant and asked all sorts of questions about my life and my job. I was cool as a cu-

cumber when Dr. Davis came in. He was wearing his magnifying dermatologist glasses like a dork. I loved him immediately.

What I wasn't expecting was the hotter than crap resident shadowing the good doctor that day to come sailing in behind him.

Of course.

Dr. Davis introduced Dr. Hotness to me. A sound burst forth from my throat that was something like a "Haaahhhhhhiiiiiaaaahhhh?" I put a question mark at the end because my voice went up several octaves. And I became chatty. This is what always happens when I get nervous.

I was standing beside Dr. Hotness when Dr. Davis asked me to show him my rash. For three seconds I contemplated how weird it would be if I peaced out and candidly left the room, shutting the door behind me. When I realized the inevitable, my brain switched gears. I became adamant about figuring out a way to lie down on the examination table. I needed gravity to be my friend.

I played it totally chill. I casually hopped my butt up onto the table and then sort of reclined on my elbows while I lifted my shirt. Both doctors leaned in to evaluate the damage, and in my opinion they hung around for a minute too long. Finally Dr. Davis straightened and delivered his diagnosis.

Poison ivy.

The verdict seemed unlikely to me. I knew he had a medical degree, but don't you think a girl who grew up in the country her entire life would have broken out in poison ivy before if she was allergic? And if that was the case, shouldn't it have been on my hands?

For the record, I'm thankful it wasn't the psoriasis or leprosy I had dreaded earlier in the week. I decided to stick with my self-diagnosis of shingles.

Dr. Davis asked me if I may have come in contact with the plant recently. I told him I had been cutting branches from trees with my dad, but it wasn't as though I'd been wearing a belly shirt. My midriff, I said, hadn't seen the light of day for fifteen years.

That's when Dr. Hotness stifled a laugh.

What was I saying? I was acting like an idiot. I started joking about my milky white coloring, and I may have compared the skin on my abdomen to the consistency of veal.

Could someone staple my mouth shut, please?

Dr. Hotness continued to smile. That adorable, lovely smile with those perfect teeth. Dr. Davis asked if I wanted topical cream or oral medicine. I explained that I had pretty much tried everything. Then I looked directly at Dr. Hotness for some reason and said, "I'll take whatever you have to give."

Dear reader. As the words exited my mouth, my ears heard them and transmitted all sorts of messages to my brain to shut up, shut up, shut up, shut up. But it was too late. Dr. Hotness shook his head in pity and turned to leave the room so he could properly feel sorry for me with dismal facial expressions.

And then I broke out in hives. From my neck all the way up to my cheeks. It was so bad the nurse asked me if I was okay.

Yeah. I'm okay, I thought. *I'm going to be over here slowly rocking back and forth. Pay no attention to the oddball in the corner with phantom shingles.*

But I managed not to say, "Do you mind giving the hot doctor my number? I'd like to use my mulligan."

24

Paging Dr. McDreamy

Exactly one month after my bout with phantom shingles, I experienced something I had never experienced as a single person: a hospital stay.

An appendectomy was not covered in my Single Life Emergency Plan. I had my tornado spot, an escape route for fires, a plan in case the house was broken into by robbers, and a hiding place should the need arise. I even designated a chair where I'd perform the Heimlich maneuver on myself if necessary.

Hospitalization, however, never occurred to me. There was an appendix-sized hole in my plan.

It all started with a general "blah" feeling. Nothing sounded good for dinner. I felt lethargic. All I wanted to do was take a bath. And go to sleep, so I did. Or at least I tried. A miserable stomachache kept me awake. After two or three hours, I begged my body to expel something. I didn't care which end it came out. I no longer wanted to be the host of this hideous beast.

Writhing in pain soon turned into frantically searching the internet for the signs of food poisoning. I suspected the tacos from a food truck were the delinquents of my plight. I stretched. I soaked in another bath. I crumbled into the fetal position. I was hot. I was cold. I was exhausted.

Rebecca called the following morning. She switched into mothering mode and wisely instructed me to go to a medical center since it was Saturday. I had been in pain for roughly twelve hours. There was no end in sight, so I listened.

I learned the phrase "abdominal pain" is vague enough to make all the staff in the front office of a medical center take bets that you're pregnant and not ready to accept the life-altering reality of the situation. I told two nurses and one doctor that unless human babies have advanced to a ten-year gestation period, there was no way I was with child unless I had been artificially inseminated during my last well-woman exam, which had been a year ago. The team did not think my *Jane the Virgin* joke was funny and insisted I pee into a cup to be sure.

It was infuriating. No, I was *not* pregnant. Then it turned depressing. No, I was not pregnant.

The doctor kept poking me in the lower right quadrant of my middle, asking if the pain was in that spot. It wasn't. The pain was right below my belly button and getting worse. Considering I was not running a fever or throwing up, I was discharged once my pregnancy test came back negative.

Doctors can't diagnose a patient when all they have to go on is, "The devil's fire is in my belly. *Do something!*"

Before I left, the doctor warned me to drive myself immediately to the hospital if I developed a fever. Cue me driving myself to an urgent care center in my neighborhood exactly two hours later. Once again I found myself assuring a team of medical assistants I was not pregnant. They made me pee into a cup, too, even though

I offered to go back to the medical center I had previously visited to retrieve my negative test results out of their trash can.

After several hours, the doctor confirmed my pain was from appendicitis, and I needed to go to a hospital immediately. The medical community does not joke around with this irritable little organ. If it's mad, we need to remove it *now*.

I sat in a cold exam room, shaking. That's when Rebecca walked in, followed by Ranelle and Lara. I may have cried. Now I had three friends debating which other hospital I should go to, which left my brain free to concentrate on not throwing up.

The doctor made me ride all alone in an ambulance to Methodist Hospital two miles down the road. It was a sketchy time for me. In that ten minutes, I convinced myself my appendix was spewing poisonous goo into my gut. There wasn't anyone there to tell me otherwise.

They wheeled me into my room where Ranelle, Rebecca, and Lara were waiting. At this point I tried to be calm, knowing I was about to go under the knife for emergency surgery, and all I could think about was whether I would be able to write my post for *Entertainment Weekly* that Thursday.

Oh sweet Pre-Appendectomy Lincee. You are adorable.

A resident walked in, pulled up my hospital gown, and started poking my mid-region. He was young and convinced the pain was not from my appendix. He started throwing around scary words like *colon* and *cervix* and *bowels*. This made me super nervous. I probably would have started crying again had the hot guy not walked into my room.

Not once did I consider the fact that I had not washed my hair in days and still had remnants of makeup from Friday morning on my face. I had not brushed my teeth either. Hygiene hadn't been a priority when I was trying not to pass out from pain that morning. We were pushing midnight on Saturday, and this guy was a breath of fresh air. We called him Dr. Boots because he wore cowboy boots with his scrubs. He was extremely attractive and all up in my abdo-men, rooting around with the resident.

What is the deal with my mid-region attracting hot doctors?

The resident was eager to share his findings with Dr. Boots, who gave him a "simmer down" look before he said they needed to check my scans from the ER. He came back fast, with a big smirk on his face.

> DR. BOOTS: "Have you ever had your abdomen scanned before?"
>
> ME: "Nope."
>
> DR. BOOTS: "Well, we figured out why you aren't sore. Your appendix isn't in the right place."
>
> ME: "I knew I was special."
>
> DR. BOOTS: "And your colon is backward too."
>
> ME: "So you're saying I'm extra special?"
>
> DR. BOOTS: "Let's get you up to surgery."
>
> ME: "I want you to do it. You know things, and I feel we've bonded."
>
> DR. BOOTS (LAUGHING): "I'll be assisting the surgeon. Don't you worry."
>
> ME: "Do they let you wear your cowboy boots in surgery?"

I blame my side of the conversation on lack of sleep and food, coupled with severe pain.

I was wheeled off to surgery, where I sat forever waiting for the random surgeon to arrive. You know, the one who was going to split me open and dig around organs that were apparently in disarray to find the buggy little one insisting on ruining my writing schedule.

The anesthesiologist was a nice lady who tried to put my raw nerves at ease, but I still felt scared. I told her I was anxious about going under. I also didn't want to stay in the hospital by myself. I started to cry, thinking about how there wouldn't be anyone at my apartment to help nurse me back to health. I explained that I didn't have a husband or children.

She was concerned for me. Not in a sweet way, but more of a "this lady is about to have a meltdown" way. She slipped me a little happy juice to calm me down. Or shut me up. I can't be sure.

Before I knew it, I was being wheeled back into my room after surgery. It was the middle of the night, it had been a long day, and my friends were there waiting for me. I should have been overwhelmed with gratitude and thanksgiving. Instead, I kept asking, "Where are my panties?"

Rebecca, who has a husband, four children, and lives a good forty-five minutes away, spent the rest of the night with me on a fold-out cot. We were both startled when the nurse barged into the room every thirty minutes to take my vitals or those of the tiny, old Filipino woman on the other side of the dividing curtain. I decided to call her Kimmy.

Kimmy may have been physically alone, but she was never digitally alone. She had an all-access Skype pass to Southeast Asia and talked to members of her family all the livelong day. Rebecca and I ignored our opportunity to wish Kimmy's relatives a "happy birthday" or "happy anniversary" in the wee hours of the morning.

Caroline showed up at the crack of dawn to relieve Rebecca. I was aware of this switch-off, but I don't remember much else, other than Caroline taking pictures of us to send to Stephanie. We were all roommates together at Baylor, and Caroline deemed this a perfect "Sic 'Em Bears" photo op.

It seemed as though every time I opened my eyes, another person was there and I kept repeating, "Where's Caroline?"

It's important to note I was obsessed with Caroline's whereabouts. Ninety-nine percent of the time, Caroline was sitting right beside me. Most of the girls who drifted in and out were from my church, and I was anxious that Caroline might feel left out because she didn't know any of them. I was trying to play hostess in my drugged-out state.

"Where's Caroline?" definitely rivaled the perpetual "Where are my panties?" question that insisted on floating out of my mouth every five seconds.

Look, it's not that I cared about these panties. This was straight-up curiosity. I went into surgery with panties. I came out without them. Did someone throw them away? Did they have to be cut off? Did something embarrassing I don't remember happen? Y'all, I could not let it go.

I also scratched myself silly. I'm mildly allergic to anesthesia, and every time I've been under, I've come out the other side burning like a mad woman. My arms, knees, ankles, and belly itch the worst. And my throat. I also fight sleep. My body screams for me to stay awake while my brain makes a compromise and allows one eye to shut.

Let me recap so you can fully appreciate this mental picture: grown woman in a hospital gown, scratching every inch of uncovered skin, one eye closed, with wild, greasy hair asking, "Where's Caroline?" and "Where are my panties?" on repeat through the white noise of Filipino Skype conversations.

Somewhere on Hinge, this exact image is some dude's profile pic.

During my ordeal, one of the girls made the executive decision to call Mama and tell her I was a little worse for wear. This appendectomy was kicking my butt. Mama hightailed it from Hallsville to Houston, and my friends Ann and Amy drove to my apartment to pick her up so she wouldn't have to negotiate the medical complex chaos. All parties involved thought this was a brilliant plan. While Ann and Amy did that, Caroline, Natalie, and Emily encouraged me to eat.

Without a doubt, the key to a successful appendectomy is passing gas and pooping as soon as possible afterward. No less than five people will ask you thirty-seven times a day if you have passed gas or had a bowel movement. It's a middle school boy's dream. You obviously eat food to make that happen. But when you have a stomach full of evil surgery gas, and it basically hurts to be alive, the last thing you want is a sandwich from the hospital menu.

Mama arrived in full force. She had packed a bag, brought a pillow, and was kind enough to share her deodorant with her daughter. She charmed her way into a pair of hospital socks, added a few extra blankets, and set up shop in the recliner with her magazine. I, on the other hand, was going on day three with zero sleep. At one point I thought about consulting the Google to translate phrases from Kimmy's side of the curtain so I could share in whatever story Bagong (her sister) reported from the opposite side of the world. Mama complained about our room being the temperature of a meat locker to anyone with a pulse. Who was burning up hot? *This girl.*

At least I had a thunderstorm to watch while I concentrated on passing gas.

Ah, yes. The thunderstorm. My appendix decided to wig out when a devastating flood hit Houston. Nobody could get into the city. Nobody could get out. I'll let you imagine the demeanor of the poor hospital staff who were stuck in a germy building with a Filipino Skype addict, a skinny woman with zero body heat, and a crazy patient whose goal in life was to poop.

I sent out a text to everyone asking them to *pray for poop.* Of course, I included the smiling poo emoji because tact and sanity had gone out the window with my hygiene. I was on the verge of a nervous breakdown, and I needed some good news other than Kimmy's son getting a promotion at work.

The next morning Mama called the hospital cafeteria. This seemed like the perfect time to try to force a turkey club down my gullet. And maybe some prune juice to get my system kicking? Two hours later my food arrived. A darling candy striper carried it in and profusely apologized that, due to the recent flooding, cafeteria workers were few and far between. We would have to eat what we were served.

I kid you not, dear reader. Green beans were on that plate. Mama was beside herself. All they needed was a little salt.

This is what we call kicking a girl while she's down.

Mama fed me bits of a roll, which tasted like pennies, and a lemon ice slush drink, which also tasted like pennies. We took a stroll with my IV pole around the floor and visited the nurse friends we had bonded with in the last forty-eight hours. I hadn't had this much fun since that church lock-in in junior high.

As I crawled back into my bed, a resident walked in to check on me. His name was Dr. Matt, and he was literally one of the most attractive men I had ever met. Seriously, borderline beautiful.

I was on day three and a half sans shower, watching as this hunk lifted my gown to get all up in my grill. I only thought, "Between Dr. Matt and Dr. Boots, we need to have a *Bachelor* casting call at Methodist Hospital." He was incredibly funny, polite, and said what every girl wants to hear:

DR. MATT: "You look good!"
LINCEE: "You look good too!"

What am I saying?

DR. MATT: "Why, thank you. You can go home this evening if you feel up to it."
LINCEE: "You are my favorite person in the world. Don't tell Dr. Boots I said that."

Within seconds, Mama had packed up everything in sight. She was eager to feel the sun again. I was so excited, I tried to carry on a conversation with Kimmy as I walked like an old lady to the bathroom. "I'm going home!" She had no idea what I was saying, but she told her family member something in response via Skype. I trust it was more colorful than, "That white girl stinks" or "I wonder if she ever found Caroline?"

Hours later we finally received my release orders. My nurse sent for a wheelchair. That's when it occurred to me that neither my mom nor I had a car. No problem. I called the troops to see if someone could come get us.

Okay, one small problem: the flooding prevented anyone from making it to my side of Houston.

Of course.

Do you think that stopped me? No way. This is what Uber is for, right? I consulted my app as Mama kept asking me, "What's You-Ber? Can we trust You-Ber? Is that the driver's last name? You-Ber?"

The Uber driver called to say he would not be rushing all the way to Methodist only to take me four miles down the road to my apartment. Of course. We called a taxi instead and hospital person-nel wheeled me away.

Bye, Kimmy! Call me, Dr. Matt!

As we reached the elevators, another nurse scurried up to us. "This was in your file! You almost forgot it." It was a biohazard bag. The one they use for blood samples.

Holding my long-lost panties.

25

It Takes a Village

When we arrived at my apartment, I walked to my door bent over like a Disney witch. I was up most of that night, moving from a chair to the couch and back to the chair again. No poop. No sleep. Even water still tasted like pennies.

Right when I was about to accept bodily functions were never going to go my way, I felt a sensation in my gut an awful lot like a lighter version of the appendix pain.

My first thought: *Did they not really take it out?*

My second thought: *Could this be my backward colon acting up now?*

My third thought: *Perhaps this is the onset of pooping!*

Something was about to happen. I could tell. My sister happened to call while I waited for the bowel movement. Once again, we were in ride-or-die mode. I commanded her to distract me with tales from the outside. When she shared an anecdote that made me laugh big time, I doubled over in pain. She felt bad, but not really. She continued the story, and I had no choice but to adjust my laugh into something throaty and annoying. It was the only way to survive her humor.

Then it happened. I pooped. I celebrated. Mama celebrated. Jamie took credit for the blessed event. It was a good day.

Sadly, sleep still eluded me. I paced back and forth with my hunched posture, willing my body to relax. Mama left the next day, probably because she was so embarrassed that her daughter stocked her kitchen with Dr Pepper, cheese, pickles, Pringles, and Oreos instead of kitchen gadgets and utensils. Pay no attention to the fact that I use my oven as storage.

Lara came over that night, and when I opened the door, I could tell she was going to secretly text an SOS message to Team I Hate Green Appendix, reporting that I was a maniac going on five days of no sleep and was severely dehydrated from metal mouth.

She took matters into her own hands, called a doctor friend, and secured an appointment for the next morning. My friend Terri drove me to the office, and within minutes the doctor determined it would be best if I was readmitted to the hospital for tests. Just to be safe.

After crying on Terri's shoulder, I collected myself. We were told to go to the hospital and that they would be waiting for us. I would have driven straight there, but Terri is not as much of a rule-follower as I am. We went to my apartment first so I could get some stuff. She told me to pack a change of clothes, which I thought was weird, but I obeyed and packed them anyway.

Three hours later, I was wheeled to a private room back on the eighth floor at Methodist. Where was Dr. Boots? What about Dr. Matt? Hey, Kimmy!

The first nurse came into my room and asked if it was okay if some students drew my blood. Who am I to deny these precious girls a future in nursing? I agreed, but I also informed them I am a hard stick. The girls were giddy. They were both up for a challenge and got to work assessing my arms.

Five sticks later, the actual nurse stepped in to show the little babies how it's done. She couldn't draw blood from my veins either.

It was time to page Big Ben.

Big Ben is a legend. Rumor has it that he can draw blood from a stone. He started the process by thawing my fingers in very warm blankets. My hands, in his expert opinion, were too cold to manipulate. I had to sit there and bake for thirty minutes. In the meantime, my friend Connie and not my attorney cousin but another friend, Stephanie, bounced into the room. Those two combined with Terri made for some gloriously miserable moments of me saying, "Stop! It hurts to laugh!" All concurred that my adopted chuckle was incredibly obnoxious, but they agreed to wait until I was out of the hospital to properly make fun of me. Also, Stephanie brought me some booty wipes. Best gift ever.

Seriously, make note. For your next hospital stay, bring booty wipes. Or ask Stephanie to bring you some. They were a game changer.

Terri left me in the capable hands of Connie and Stephanie. Big Ben rolled in an ultrasound machine since homegirl here has invisible veins. He stuck and stuck and came up with zilch. Stephanie, who is a nurse, was on the brink of doing it herself when another nurse came in as calm as can be. She asked, "Has anyone taken your blood yet?" We all laughed. Three hours had gone by and no one had succeeded, although six people had tried.

Nurse Calm Cool and Collected walked up to me, patted my arm a couple of times, stuck me, and yawned as the blood began to flow. Say hello to the new Big Ben, people!

My friend Catha joined the party minutes later. She was assigned the lovely task of spending the night with me in yet another recliner. We chatted for a few hours about everything under the sun. That's right. Hours. My nurse walked in to say my blood test results came back with low potassium levels. Instead of offering me a banana, she set me up with a potassium drip. As she attached it to my port, she mentioned, "Now, this is probably going to hurt."

It felt like molasses slowly coursing through my arm. I became restless. Catha did her best to distract me, but I had to keep my arm perfectly straight to keep the machine from beeping. After thirty minutes, I couldn't stand it anymore. The nurse turned down the amount of potassium, explaining that it was going to take longer to enter my system now. I was on that drip from 10:00 p.m. to 4:00 a.m. At one point they shoved ice packs around my arm to numb the pain. As Catha slept (not really), I watched old episodes of *Friends*. That's what I do in times of distress.

Could this appendectomy *be* any more annoying?

Catha left at five o'clock in the morning because my friends have jobs and traffic in Houston can suck the life out of you. Ranelle was slated to arrive around 7:30. After the evil potassium drip dropped its last bit of nutrients into my body, I fell asleep. Thirty minutes later, my nurse woke me up to say she was leaving.

I was confused. Did she need me to affirm her service? Should I write a thank-you note? Was she expecting a tip? She introduced me to the new guy who would be taking her place. Both asked me if I had passed gas or had a bowel movement. Both reminded me it would be a good idea for me to go ahead and do that.

I smiled and thanked them instead of scratching their eyes out.

Suddenly my surgeon and Dr. Matt walked in to see why the heck I was back in the hospital. I don't remember how I answered, but I do remember reasoning that Dr. Matt and I have a solid foundation with which to build our relationship. He has seen me at my worst. Crazy hair, no bra, prickly leg hair, less-than-minty breath, track marks up and down my arms from multiple needle sticks. I grinned at him, figuring he knew it was all downhill from there.

My surgeon lifted my gown to admire his work. Dr. Matt shoved his nose in there too. The surgeon began pressing hard on my abdomen to make sure my insides were as they should be. He was right around my belly button when he asked if I was in any pain.

> ME: "Maybe you should stop poking me before I answer."

Dr. Matt laughed. He tried to hold it together in front of his boss, but I rejoiced in my victory. Dr. Matt thinks I'm funny! Only one thing could tear my eyes away from his beautiful forearms.

> SURGEON: "We're going to release you."
> ME: "Hooray!"
> SURGEON: "After we get a stool sample, of course. You've had a bowel movement, right?"
> ME: "Yes. Yes I have."
> DR. MATT: "Today?"
> ME: "You know me so well, Dr. Matt. No. Not today."

My surgeon and Dr. Matt left me so I could have a serious talk with my digestive system. My male nurse came in to deposit a delightful little BM tray in my bathroom. I debated calling my good luck poop charm, but I knew my sister was teaching at her school and wouldn't be able to coax anything out of me.

Then it hit me. The feeling was small, but it was there. I was ready to pass gas. The anticipation was killing me, so I gave a little guttural push to help things along. Only gas didn't come out.

I hopped up from my bed, grabbed my IV pole, and sprinted like an ambitious snail to the bathroom. I evaluated the damage in the full-length mirror.

Have you ever changed a baby's diaper and genuinely wondered out loud, "Now, how did it get all the way up there?" Visualize that scenario on a grown woman.

I removed my gown and underthings and placed them directly into the trash can. I used half a box of booty wipes to clean myself up, swinging between audible laughs and tears. As I stood naked in the bathroom, it occurred to me that All-Knowing Terri forced me to pack extra clothes. My panties were on the other side of the door, but the likelihood that my male nurse or the woman who took my vitals every thirty minutes would waltz in and see me in all my glory was high. Worse, what if Dr. Matt stopped by to ask me out?

I called Ranelle for an ETA. She was in the parking garage. I calmly explained that current circumstances were grim, and she responded that she was on her way. As I waited, nude in the bathroom, holding on to my IV pole, that now familiar sensation hit me again. Only this time, it was an explosion of bodily functions. My celebration was cut short when I saw my BM tray sitting on the shelf by the sink. I had wasted my one chance to blow this joint by pooping in the toilet like a civilized person.

Ranelle walked in and secured a new hospital gown from an orderly and underwear from my bag. I was extremely woozy, and Ranelle had to help me figure out how to put on a hospital gown while tethered to an IV pole. Welcome to the precise point when Ranelle and I became "those" friends. If you've seen someone's business and helped her discard soiled linens in the proper bin without hospital staff noticing, you've reached a pinnacle of friendship no Hallmark card will ever be able to touch.

As long as I've been appendix free, I swear I can feel my food digest. Friends in the medical community insist I'm crazy, but I know my body. My belly button is a bit janky, which makes me uptight, but I can live with it. Dr Pepper tastes like Dr Pepper again, which makes me happy.

I'm thankful my appendix did not burst. I am equally humbled by an army of friends who stopped everything to help me in my time of need. They cooked, cleaned, purchased every food item from

H-E-B to stock my refrigerator, did laundry, ran errands, drove me to appointments, and checked on me multiple times a day. I felt comforted, cared for, and embraced.

I may not have a husband, but I do have a village. And I love each one of you.

26

I Feel the Need. The Need for Speed Dating.

Stop what you're doing and think back to everything you've ever heard about speed dating. Use your imagination. Do you have the mental picture? Do you see yourself? Can you envision the man across the table?

Aaaaannnnnndddd it is as awkward as you are imagining. Allow me to embellish.

My friend Catherine somehow managed to convince me speed dating was an exercise we should check off our single gal bucket list. I don't remember why I agreed, but it's clear now that I suffered through the uncomfortable experience so you wouldn't have to. You're welcome.

We arrived at the speed-dating lounge exactly on time. We were looking fabulous and feeling good. Our lips were glossy, our smiles were sparkling, and if we had been honest with each other, we would have had to admit our armpits were beginning to glisten in expectation of what interesting turn of events the evening might bring.

We made our way cautiously across the scantily filled bar and spied the designated speed-dating staging area, complete with little numbered cards on each table. Our heads turned back to the entrance when we noticed no one seemed to be in charge. Surely there would be a superfun official speed date greeter, right? Perhaps a table with a sign-up sheet and a complimentary breath mint?

Bemused, Catherine and I awkwardly stood around and waited for someone who looked ready to walk us through the process. No such person arrived. We opted to take a load off on bar stools, and I became somewhat relieved that this modern-day meet and greet was more than likely going to be canceled.

Just as my butt was beginning to relax, the barmaid scattered a box of name tags in front of my ice cold Dr Pepper and instructed us to find our John Hancock. I was astonished when all the people I thought were casual Friday night lounge patrons shoved Catherine over to grab their badges.

The entire lounge was there to speed date. Butt reclenched, I said a quick prayer asking the Lord to help me get through this.

Our barmaid/speed-dating hostess (I shall call her Judy) was dressed in all black. She carried an old-fashioned bell cooks ding when an order is ready at a diner. She looked like she'd rather be having a mammogram than hand-holding a bunch of rookie speed daters.

Judy: "Okay, I need the ladies to take a seat at the marked tables. When the bell rings, you will stay seated as the men rotate around. We will do this ten rounds for eight minutes apiece. Are you ready?" *Ding!*

In front of me was a card with a line for me to write down a name, a blank space for me to take notes, and a box for me to literally check yes or no. Boy, Chance was way ahead of his game when he passed me a note with this exact same layout in first grade.

First up was Ted. He was a nervous laugher.

> ME: "Hi Ted!"
> TED: "Hahahahahahaha. Hi.
> Heeheeheeheeheehee."

Hoo boy. Being a realist, I decided to get the obvious out in the open.

> ME: "So. Here we are. Speed dating. Did you ever see yourself here?"
> TED: "Hahahahahahaha. No. Heeheeheeheeheehee."
> ME: "What do you do for a living?"
> TED: "Hahahahahahaha. Chemical engineer. Heeheeheeheeheehee."

It was mainly a one-sided conversation. Poor Ted never asked a single question. I wondered how long he would sit through a pregnant pause, so I gave it a whirl. I counted to thirty before Judy's bell rang. *Ding!*

Ted laughed and then thanked me, moving on to the next table. I raised my eyes to Catherine right as she took a sip of her wine, toasting her first guy, who was moving on to my table.

Ding!

His name was Jason.

> ME: "Hi, Jason!"
> JASON: "How do you spell your name? L-I-N-C-E-E? That's weird."
> ME: "Yep. But I'm not weird. I'm pretty cool."

I paused for laughter. There was no laughter.

JASON: "What do you do for fun?"

ME: "Great question. I like to go to the movies, dance, spend time with my friends, write, read . . ."

JASON: "What are you reading?"

I opted not to admit a well-worn *People* magazine was on my bedside table. I needed to make a good impression. I decided to reveal the last book I read.

ME: *"Prince of Tides.* What are you reading?"

JASON: *"Third Reich."*

Dear reader. It took all that was in me not to look him directly in the eyes and inquire if he was looking for a woman to bear his Aryan children.

ME: "Oh! You're a history buff, huh? What's your favorite book of all time?"

JASON: *"Lord of the Rings.* Have you read it?"

ME: "Yes, I have."

JASON: "Not watched it. *Read it."*

ME (RATHER COOLLY): "Yes. I have."

Amazed that I had read anything other than the Hunger Games, Harry Potter, and Twilight sagas, Jason suddenly became interested in my potential. After all, I do have blond hair and light eyes. With a little spark and excitement in his voice, he went on.

JASON: "Have you ever read *Dune?*"

ME: "Doom?"

JASON (EXASPERATED): "No. *Dune*. D-U-N-E."
ME: "No. N-O."

I kid you not. This dude marked something in his booklet about me in the little notes section. Without a doubt Jason checked the no box. He would have used a Sharpie if Judy had supplied him one. The people pleaser in me wanted to stop Jason and start rattling off statistics about *Star Wars* and the Dagobah system and planet Hoth, but I stopped myself. Jason had made his decision, and I needed to respect that.

Ding!

The next few speed-dating delegates were a bit on the vanilla side. I kept trying to spark a funny conversation or make one of them laugh, but it never happened. I was so close to asking one dude if he had ever kissed a girl, but Judy interrupted by ringing her bell. She reminded us we were halfway through this super fun night on the town. *Ding!*

ME: "Hi, Mel. I'm Lincee."
MEL: "Hi. Do you mind if I write some notes down about the other girls? I haven't had time and I don't want to forget anything."

By all means, Mel. I'm a writer as well.

I smiled blankly at him. I noticed they had dimmed the lights, and we all seemed a bit more mysterious from the soft glow of votive candles. If they ignored the table numbers, Judy's bell, and the homework in front of us, innocent onlookers might easily theorize we were all in romantic rendezvous. I glanced over at Catherine. She was having a fabulous time. She is so good at stuff like this. I looked back at Mel. He was craning his neck to read my friend's name tag.

ME: "Her name is Catherine."

MEL: "Do you know if it's with a C or with a K?"

ME: "With a C!"

MEL: "Thanks! Okay, I'm done. So . . ."

Ding! Nice talking to you, Mel.

With careful swagger, Giovanni made his way to my table. If a Houston version of *Jersey Shore* existed, he would have been the star. Oozing confidence in his jet-black satin shirt unbuttoned to his navel, Giovanni swooped in and used the age-old rule of complimenting above the neck.

GIOVANNI: "You have the most amazing teeth."

ME: "Why, thank you."

GIOVANNI: "And you accessorize beautifully. I love your necklace."

ME: "Wanna borrow it?"

Giovanni also complimented my dress. The green brought out my eyes. Note to self. For the next seven minutes and thirty seconds, Giovanni raved about his hair, his grandmother's meatballs, and his car dealership. I've never wanted to hear a bell ring so badly in my entire life.

Ding!

Josh sat down.

JOSH: "So? How's your mother?"

I was confused for a split second and then giggled. Finally! Someone with a sense of humor. Sadly, Josh's potential crashed and burned after the halfway mark. He was screaming at me and boisterously laughing at his own jokes. I decided he had a hearing impairment.

His voice was a little off and it took effort to form his words. Maybe he was afraid he wouldn't be able to hear me? That's why he rambled on about himself. As he left my table, I leaned over to Catherine and asked if he talked to her.

CATHERINE: "Yes, but I could hardly understand him."

ME: "Because of the hearing impairment?"

CATHERINE: "Uh, no. Because he was drunk."

Undeniably, I need to get out more.

Number of engineers? Six.

Number of guys openly obsessed with *Battlestar Galactica*? Three.

Impending totalitarian dictator? One.

Enough material for a future book? Priceless.

I laugh it off, but at the end of the day I still have to confront the sting of rejection that hides in the deep corners and crevices of my heart. I will admit the odds of my meeting Mr. Right in an eight-minute round of speed dating were slim to none.

Of course, I wasn't interested in Giggling Ted or the *Lord of the Rings* guy. I didn't see myself with Giovanni or Mel. But there is always that small sliver of hope. The one that whispers, "This might be it."

I like to lean into that hope.

My friend Dennis announced to me one day that he was going to write about *The Notebook* on his blog. I begged him to tread lightly, because this classic romance is sacred territory. He laughed, accepted my warning as a challenge, and posted a scathing review about a movie I have held close to my heart since 2004.

Then he did something unconventional. He flipped everything around and recapped the movie again, channeling his inner, softer side. It was a sweet pile of lovey-dovey goodness with a cherry on top. I was not expecting that. He used phrases like "love language" and "dedicating his existence" and "fulfilled and smitten heart."

He insightfully ended with this gem: "The larger picture is that true love never dies and that every woman wants to feel as loved and secure as Allie ultimately ended up feeling."

I paused to have a nostalgic Carrie Bradshaw moment. My computer faced a beige wall with a bulletin board full of haphazard Post-it notes instead of a quaint New York City street on the Upper East Side, but you get my drift. The electricity in the air was still the same as I dictated a question to myself.

Are we setting ourselves up for disappointment when we cling to hope?

In a tender scene in *The Notebook*, Noah's head finally figures out what his heart has been telling him all along—Allie is special. In a time when chivalry was nowhere near dead, the only way he could hold her in the most gentlemanly way possible was to ask her to dance.

I love that Allie answers, "Sure." Oh how I identify with this part of her character.

Noah leads her to an empty street and assumes the standard dance position, humming a few bars of the most romantic tune he knows. I admire Allie's gumption as she informs him he is a terrible singer. He humbly accepts her critique and pulls her closer. Then she compliments him, because what is happening in front of her eyes is special. Guys don't spontaneously dance with girls in the middle of the street as they gently sway to Billie Holiday crooning in the background. He pulls away for a dip. She smiles, because every girl feels light as a feather when she's dipped. He brings her close again, and you can see he is done. There's no going back. Allie is his life now, and he will stop at nothing to make her realize he is the only one for her.

Nicholas Sparks wrote the book from which those scenes were born. Countless artists on my iTunes account sing lyrics with similar sentiments. Hallmark dedicates an entire channel to people who stumble across their soul mates when they randomly end up in a tiny Midwestern town whose residents are obsessed with Christmas.

I cling to hope because I choose not to live in despair.

I know life isn't a perfect reflection of a romantic comedy or power ballad, but my desire to love and be loved with all my heart will always be there. I believe in romance. I believe two people can fall for each other on opposite sides of a screen. I believe in checking the yes box.

I lean on the hope that somewhere out there, a guy is going to find me captivating. And I can't wait.

A boom box held over his head. A ride on a lawn mower into the sunset. A meeting at the top of the Empire State Building. A birthday cake on a glass dining room table. A "Sissy" license plate in the rear window of his truck. Risking his life to save me from the lightning sand. A glass slipper that happens to be size eight. A perfectly timed laugh. A touch at the small of my back. The gaze that says it all.

A simple dance in the street.

Reflections

Keri was the one who suggested I face my insecurities head-on. My dear friend graciously listened as I flipped out over a bridesmaid dress. The color was beautiful. The length was perfect. The material was divine. But the sleeves were missing. My jiggling arms would be exposed in front of the entire church. What was I going to do?

She proposed we memorize Scripture.

I admit, my brain did not go in that direction. I expected her to suggest I check Pinterest for an aggressive tricep workout or research the cost of liposuction. Instead, Keri forced me to focus upward instead of inward. She recommended we learn Psalm 139 together.

The wedding was in twenty-four days. Psalm 139 has twenty-four verses. Coincidence? Or divine intervention?

Keri understood that I struggled with body image issues. She also knew this was the first time I would be participating in a wedding since my divorce, and the only way I could control my emotions was with truth.

Psalm 139 is now my go-to chapter when I'm feeling insecure. Each verse is packed with unwavering confidence, assuring me that the Lord knows me personally. It also claims,

You created my inmost being; you knit me together in my mother's womb. I will praise you because I am fearfully and wonderfully made; your works are wonderful, I know that full well. (vv. 13–14)

I am definitely a work in progress, and I am constantly rewiring my heart so I don't rely on approval from my friends, Batman, hot doctors, my editors, my readers, the Dallas Cowboys, an imaginary future husband, my parents, the community of Hallsville, or social media. I know I won't find peace from the image in the mirror, a number on the scale, hits on my website, clicks from posts, the amount in my bank account, the American Girl doll store, or green beans.

My identity is in Christ. I offer Him all I have and all of who I am. I pray He continues to develop me, and that I will claim the characteristics He has placed in me that go beyond my insecurities.

She loves the Lord.

She has a servant's heart.

She can dance.

She is kind.

She is passionate.

She has a faithful spirit.

She can make a mean banana pudding.

She is a fierce friend.

Her words are powerful.

And yes, she hates green beans.

I see you. I know your struggle. God sees you. His love is real. And He will always hold you in the palm of His hand.

Acknowledgments

I would like to thank so many people for their part in making this book a reality. These are the individuals who prayed, provided encouragement and/or oxygen when needed, spoke truth, prayed again, and fed me Mexican food when the going got dicey. I am forever grateful for each and every one:

Caroline Applegate, Susan Barrett, Pam Boehm, Lindsay Chernosky, Amy Cooper, Ann Corrigan, Alex Eisenhuth, Keri Engle, Emily Fraker, Connie Haugneland, Catha Jaynes, Stephanie Johnson, Terri Langford, Nancy Jane McMillan, Paula Meyers, Dennis and Danielle Postiglione, Angel Texada, Elizabeth Williams, and Bill Wright.

Thanks to Angela Sostre and Kathryn Luttner for trusting me with a very big platform with which to write.

A big round of applause to Kelsey Bowen, Brittany Miller, and all the folks at Revell for owning this project. Could this group be any cooler?

Lisa Jackson, your ability to read my thoughts is uncanny. Thank you for being my _____. (*Text me your answer. I want to see if you were thinking what I was thinking when I wrote this!*)

Where Melanie Shankles leads, I will follow. Anthropologie, a speaking engagement, Kyle Field, church, Target . . . I'm there.

I'd like to thank my spirit animal, our host Chris Harrison, for coming into my life back in March 2002. It's been quite a journey full of ups and downs, but it's been equally amazing. Will you accept this rose?

Julie Medford has been there with me since we were fifteen years old. I don't see that changing. She's the original chop to my suey.

Natalie Weakly taught me to hope in Psalm 20:4–5. It was a game changer.

I wouldn't be sane without Ranelle Woolrich in my life. I hope you find your own Ranelle one day.

The good Lord knew what He was doing when He introduced me to Stephanie Holstead. Although we've only known each other for a handful of years, it feels like she's always been right there. She's *the most* fun!

I had the privilege of living with Lara Pringle while I was writing this book. Even though she has eyewitness accounts of my "every day is pajama day" phase, I will cherish the times she encouraged me, made me laugh, forced me to eat something other than Starburst jellybeans, and distracted me with episodes of *Poldark*.

To the readers of iHateGreenBeans.com, you are the reason this book exists. We've been through a lot together. How many times have we hidden behind a couch cushion or shouted "PINEAPPLE" at the television? My guess is too many to count. For those of you who have been with me since the email days, I salute you. None of this would be possible without your willingness to visit my little corner of the internet. Thank you for continuing to read each and every week.

I have no words to describe my special bond with Jill Hatley and Rebecca Juillerat. These women have spent decades filling me with biblical truth, which they supplemented with healthy servings of queso. I honestly could not have made it out of the trench without their kind words, brutal honesty, loud cheers, and infectious laughter. One of you is the wind beneath my left wing, and the other is the wind beneath my right. I'll let y'all fight over who's who, because deciding stuff like that makes me sweat.

If you are in my extended family, I hope the fact that I am now a published author will score me a coveted spot at the grown-up table for Thanksgiving and Christmas dinners. Also, I love you all.

Gary Eisenhuth, thank you for loving the women in your life so well.

You have my heart, Addison.

If I had to choose to share DNA with anyone in the world, it would be with my sister, Jamie Eisenhuth. She is my rock, my strength, my ambassador, and my forever friend. I finally forgive you for dangling my Strawberry Shortcake doll over the balcony.

Daddy, I'm sorry I never got you those Dallas Cowboys tickets, but in my defense, your TV screen is so big, it's as though we're there at the stadium anyway. Thank you for believing in me. I hope I've made you proud.

I love you, Mummy. Can you believe green beans got us here? You knew the entire time, didn't you? It's been your master plan from the beginning. Well done, Mama. Well done.

It's all about *You*, Jesus. With the hope that You will be glorified, I surrender these pages.

"I love you, O LORD, my strength" (Psalm 18:1).

Lincee Ray began blogging accidentally when she wrote a recap for the beloved show everyone loves to hate—*The Bachelor*. Once her audience reached triple digits, she launched her website, www .iHateGreenBeans.com. What began as a place for closeted *Bachelor* watchers to commune and discuss the wonder that is Our Host Chris Harrison slowly morphed into a place where Lincee shares stories of her everyday life.

Lincee's *Bachelor* recaps later miraculously landed on the desk of an editor at *Entertainment Weekly*. The woman quickly deduced that Lincee was a pop culture weirdo who probably watched all the teenybopper shows on The CW. She was right.

Lincee taught herself to say the ABCs backward as a child. It kills at parties. She really does hate green beans and is a little too enthusiastic about Dr Pepper and seasonal-themed Oreos. She also believes it's important to tell your stories—even the ones that make you seem a little crazy.

Connect WITH Lincee!

For more on Lincee's blog, podcast, and speaking schedule visit **iHateGreenBeans.com**.

 LinceeRay   @LinceeRay   @Lincee